HOW TO HEAR GOD'S VOICE
IN MARRIAGE

STUDY GUIDE

ZOE Ministries International
PO Box 2207
Arvada CO 80001-2207, USA
permissions@zoemin.org

Rev. 01/20

ACKNOWLEDGEMENTS

ZOE Ministries International is dedicated to training, equipping and sending believers into the world to minister by the leading of the Holy Spirit. This ministry helps build the body of Christ and encourages God's people to use their gifts and talents for His glory. It is for this purpose that this publication has been compiled by the leading of the Holy Spirit and the input of many people. ZOE Ministries wishes to thank them for their support, time, and talents in contributing to this Study Guide. We give our Lord all the praise and glory for this work!

CONTENTS

COURSE OUTLINE

Lesson 1 **INTRODUCTION**
Class Article: *God's Plan For The Home,* B. Graham

Lesson 2 **GROWING IN THE LIKENESS OF CHRIST**
Scripture: **Philippians 2:3–4; Romans 8:1–14; Galatians 5:22–26**
Wheat: Introduction and Chapter 1
Study Help: "Fruit of the Spirit—In Marriage" ZOE Ministries
Assigned Articles: *Called To Be Christ-Like,* D. Wilkerson
                    A New Heart, U.S. Grant

Lesson 3 **IN THE BEGINNING GOD CREATED**
Scripture: **Genesis 1:1–2, 26–28; Genesis 2:7, 18–25**
Wheat: Chapters 2 and 3
Assigned Articles: *Undivided: God's Plan For Couples In The Ministry,* S. and C. Benson
                    Guess What...God Knows Best, G. Stanton

Lesson 4 **COVENANT RELATIONSHIPS**
Scripture: **Hosea, Chapters 1 - 14**
Wheat: Chapter 4 and pages 228–236
Study Help: "Covenant Relationships" ZOE Ministries

Lesson 5 **LIFETIME LOVE AFFAIR**
Scripture: **Psalm 45; Proverbs 5:15–20; 1 Corinthians 7:3–5**
Wheat: Chapters 5 and 6
Assigned Article: *Love—It Never Fails,* M. Hickey
Class Worksheet: "Five Greatest Needs In Marriage" ZOE Ministries

Lesson 6 **PRESCRIPTION FOR A SUPERB MARRIAGE**
Scripture: **Song of Songs, Chapters 1 through 8**
Wheat: Chapters 12 and 13
Assigned Article: *Romancing Your Marriage,* N. Wright

Lesson 7 **TRUE ROMANCE**
Scripture: **Ephesians 5**
Wheat: Chapters 7 and 11
Assigned Articles: *Men: Date Your Wives,* E. Geiger
                    Spending Time, S. Heitzig

Lesson 8   **LET'S COMMUNICATE**

Scripture:	**James 3:1–12; Matthew 12:33-37**
Wheat:	Chapters 8 and 9
Class Worksheet:	"A Matter Of Life And Death" ZOE Ministries
Assigned Article:	*Learn From Each Other*, R. Dobbins

Lesson 9   **LET'S COMMUNICATE (CONTINUED)**

Scripture:	**Proverbs 18:21**
Study Help:	"Taming The Tongue" ZOE Ministries
Wheat:	Chapter 10
Class Role-Play:	"Let's Communicate" ZOE Ministries

Lesson 10   **FREEDOM THROUGH FORGIVENESS**

Scripture:	**Ephesians 4:26–32; Hebrews 12:14–15; Colossians 3:12–17**
Wheat:	Chapters 14 and 16
Assigned Article:	*Healing Hurting Marriages*, Dr. S. and J. King

Lesson 11   **HOW TO SAVE YOUR MARRIAGE ALONE**

Scripture:	**1 Peter 3:1–12**
Wheat:	Chapter 15, up to "The Love Story of Hosea"
Assigned Articles:	*When Church Bells Aren't Ringing*, S. Raborn
	I AM, Anonymous

Lesson 12   **SERVING GOD TOGETHER**

Scripture:	**1 Corinthians 13:1–8a**
Study Help:	"Serving God Together" ZOE Ministries
Assigned Article:	*Fundamentals Of A Christian Marriage*, Dr. J. Dobson

Study Materials:
1. Bible, any version
2. *Love Life For Every Married Couple*, Ed Wheat, M.D., Zondervan Publishing House, Grand Rapids, Michigan, 1980.
3. Various Articles in the Study Guide:
   a. Class Article—to be read in class
   b. Assigned Article—to be read in preparation for class
   c. Study Help—for the participant's use in studying at home
   d. Class Worksheet—to be used in class under the facilitator's direction

FOREWORD

Dear Participant,

We are delighted that you have been led by the Holy Spirit to go through this course on marriage. We believe that this is one of the most important courses offered by ZOE Ministries.

As you grow in your marriage, your ministry together with your spouse will soon begin to blossom. The enemy is trying very hard to destroy marriages and families, for he knows the power a couple can generate when they are in agreement. **Ecclesiastes 4:12** says, **"Though one may be overpowered, two can defend themselves. A cord of three strands is not quickly broken."** When God is placed in the center of the marriage relationship, we see strength and power that the world will want to examine.

We pray that as you study this curriculum, God will truly do signs and wonders in your lives.

God bless you, and we will be praying **Matthew 19:6, "Therefore what God has joined together, let no man separate."**

In His Service,

Dick and Ginny Chanda
Founding Directors

A NOTE TO COURSE PARTICIPANTS

What ZOE Is!

1. A ministry that provides training for disciple-making.
2. Participatory classes where all are encouraged to share and contribute.
3. A situation where the leader (facilitator) decreases and the participants increase.
4. A drawing out of ministry gifts and preparation for the Lord's calling on individual lives.
5. A time when one can grow in the understanding and appreciation of others' gifts.
6. A safe environment in which an individual can feel comfortable to practice operating in his or her gifts.
7. A time of understanding the heart of the Father and applying that to one's life.

What ZOE Is Not!

1. A traditional Bible study.
2. A class where the leader speaks and the people take notes.
3. A place where people can air their opinions or gripes.
4. A place where people can discuss church doctrines.
5. A time when "weird" ministry happens.

A Reminder to ZOE Participants:

"A ZOE course is not just a Bible study; our leader is a facilitator and coach, not a teacher."

It is our desire that the Lord Jesus Christ be glorified in all that is said and done in ZOE courses. We wish to foster an understanding of the operation of His Holy Spirit and to yield to His workings.

MAIN PRINCIPLES

Lesson 1: God has a design and purpose for every marriage, and He must be central to the marriage relationship. His help and guidance are essential for any marriage to become all He has designed it to be.

Lesson 2: We need to grow in the likeness of Christ and take this likeness into our marriage. Scripture shows us how to become the kind of spouse God wants us to be. The fruit of the Spirit can be manifested in us, enhancing our marriage.

Lesson 3: God created male and female. Each is unique, created to be different, but created for each other. God meant for man and wife to live side by side in complementary roles.

Lesson 4: A covenant is a permanent agreement involving the total being of the persons concerned. When we marry we form a blood covenant with our mate in the eyes of God. Marriage is a covenant relationship that brings with it all the benefits and responsibilities of a blood covenant.

Lesson 5: In order for us to have a lifetime love affair with our mate, we need all five aspects of love to be evident in our marriage. We must love, respect and care for our mate's body as much as we love, respect and care for our own body. As these principles are practiced in our marriage, we can remain faithful to one another.

Lesson 6: God intends that a husband and wife should enjoy sexual union within the guidelines He has given. As we choose to act and think lovingly towards our mate, trust and understanding deepens, enhancing our love relationship.

Lesson 7: There can be true romance in our marriage no matter how long or short a time we have been married. We can learn how to restore or improve the romance in our marriage.

Lesson 8: Scripture provides a warning against the evil of an uncontrolled and uncharitable tongue. Our words can either tear down our mate or bless them and build them up. We need to communicate *storge* and *phileo* love in our marriage.

Lesson 9: Scripture provides a warning against the evil of an uncontrolled and uncharitable tongue. Our words can either tear down our mate or bless them and build them up. We need to communicate *agape* love in our marriage.

Lesson 10: Forgiveness heals the marital relationship and frees us to establish a loving, healthy marriage.

Lesson 11: A marriage can be saved, even if it has only one partner who is willing to save it. Godly spouses are promised blessings from the Lord. God can empower us to become the husband and wife He wants us to be.

Lesson 12: God has a plan for our marriage and ministry together. God will reveal His plan for us as we walk in the Spirit together. He can empower us to become the husband and wife He wants us to be.

PARTICIPANT'S RESPONSIBILITIES

I. Course Preparation

A. Read the assigned scriptures and come prepared to share in the course.

1. Ask the Holy Spirit, **"Open my eyes that I may see wonderful things in your law." Psalm 119:18** You may be very familiar with the assigned Scriptures, but the Lord is very faithful and can give you "fresh manna."

2. Look at the Main Principle for the class and apply the Scriptures. Ask yourself the following questions:
   a. How does this Scripture apply to the lesson?
   b. How does this Scripture apply to my life?
   c. What do I need to do to apply this Scripture to my life and to the lives of others for God's glory?

B. Read the assigned chapters or pages in the book and come prepared to share in the course.
Note in your book any thoughts related to the Main Principle for the lesson.

C. Read the assigned articles and come prepared to share in class.
Note any thoughts related to the Main Principle for the lesson.

D. Maintain a journal—a valuable tool in God's hands.
As you learn to hear God's voice and keep a record of His speaking, you will become more aware of what He is saying to you and how He wants to work through you. See the handout "Journaling—A Good Way to Hear God's Voice."

E. Spend time in prayer.

1. Prayer is valuable preparation for these classes. The more time you spend with the Lord, the more you will come to know Him.

2. Spend time with God daily! Avoid crash studying. God shows no partiality—what He has done for others, He will do for you! Growth will come as you respond to God's Holy Spirit at work in your life.

II. Class Participation

A. Training is active! You will be encouraged to **take part in the class discussions and the prayer and ministry time.**

B. You will have the opportunity to **lead the discussion** of the assigned reading as you feel comfortable. No one will be forced to lead—only encouraged!

JOURNALING – A GOOD WAY TO HEAR GOD'S VOICE

What Goes Into a Journal?

1. Your thoughts—impressions, insights, hopes, fears, goals, struggles
2. Your feelings—both positive and negative
3. Your prayers and answers to prayer
4. Excerpts from Scripture and other reading that God seems to be highlighting for you

How To Journal

1. You may choose to use a spiral binder or a hardback blank book, or anything that you can take with you easily on trips.
2. Journal every day, if possible, during the time that you read Scripture and pray. Record in it insights that the Lord gave you that day or the day before.
3. You may want to keep a separate section in your journal for prayers or excerpts from your reading.
4. Write directly to God as if you were talking to Him or writing Him a letter.

The Benefits of Keeping a Journal Are Many

1. Journaling fosters a readiness to hear from God. Personal communion with God takes place as you write out your thoughts and feelings, and record the insights and impressions He gives you.
2. As you read God's Word and record your insights about Scripture, God is faithful to provide the admonitions, encouragement and guidance that you need.
3. Prayers become specific as you place them in print. In addition, God gets the glory when you review your journal and see your prayers have been answered.
4. Journaling helps clarify your thinking. Fears and struggles are more clearly defined so that they can be dealt with.
5. During times of discouragement, it can help to look back over your journal and see God's faithfulness and your progress in spiritual growth.

GUIDELINES FOR LEADING A COURSE DISCUSSION

1. Prayer

As you study the assigned material, ask God for insights. Ask Him to show you the main points to be discussed and questions to ask to aid the discussion. Come a few minutes early to class and pray with the Facilitators before the class begins.

2. Maintain Control of the Discussion

After the class has been turned over to you by the Facilitators, you are to maintain control of the discussion.

a. Do not allow one or two participants to dominate the discussion time.

b. Stick to the subject. God may give you many insights, but keep the discussion related to the Main Principle of the lesson.

3. Work Within the Allotted Time

For a 2 1/2 hour class:

    Approximately 30 minutes for the book

    Approximately 50 minutes for the Scripture discussion

    Approximately 15 minutes for the articles

       (Allowing 20 minutes for the Facilitators to lead the prayer/ministry)

For a 1 1/2 hour class:

    Approximately 20 minutes for the book

    Approximately 30 minutes for the Scripture discussion

    Approximately 10 minutes for the articles

       (Allowing 10 minutes for the Facilitators to lead the prayer/ministry)

ZOE courses focus on what God says through the Bible. Be careful not to spend too much time on the book or articles, which are provided only as supplements to the Scriptures.

4. Encourage Discussion

Course members should be prepared to share insights that the Lord gave them while they read the assigned material. You may need to draw out these insights by asking questions.

a. Begin with a *launch question*, a broad question that can be answered in a number of different ways by anyone in the group.

b. Then use *guide questions,* which are short questions that keep the discussion moving in a direction that is related to the Main Principle of that lesson. Life application of the principles found in the assigned reading should be a focus during some part of the discussion.

c. To close the discussion time, summarize very briefly the main points of the discussion.

May God bless you as you study and pray in preparation for the course. We will be praying for you as you prepare. We love and appreciate you.   *~The Facilitators*

LESSON 1

INTRODUCTION

MAIN PRINCIPLE

*God has a design and purpose for every marriage,
and He must be central to the marriage relationship.
His help and guidance are essential for any marriage
to become all He has designed it to be.*

DISCLAIMER

The articles that follow have been chosen to give you, the reader, a broader perspective on many of the issues presented in the course. All the ideas in these articles do not necessarily represent the views of *ZOE Ministries International*. However, we pray that as you read and study, you will glean a sense of what is in the author's heart. At all times we need to ask the question, "Does this line up with the Word of God?"

GOD'S PLAN FOR THE HOME

by Billy Graham

We know that broken homes are one of the great social problems today. Broken homes could lead to the destruction of our civilization.

The anguish and suffering that divorce brings to children caught in a situation that is not of their own making shows that we have certainly not yet reached the day when a child no longer needs both parents.

Besides divorce, there are a host of legal separations and annulments. There are thousands of homes where husband and wife continue living together, but the marriage is an endurance contest—arguing, fighting, calling each other names. Statistics don't tell of the thousands of boys and girls living in foster homes and orphanages and correctional institutions, or those living difficult lives because of broken homes.

Turn to the book of Genesis and read about the first marriage that took place. The crowning act of God's creative work is the creation of man and woman in his own image. Man finds his highest fulfillment and fellowship with God, but his nature also demands communication with his fellow man. The highest expression of human communication is the husband-wife relationship.

When my wife and I are apart because of travels, we try to keep in touch every day by telephone. Communication increases the depth of our love and increases the dependence that we have on each other and upon the Lord: "The Lord God said, 'It is not good for the man to be alone. I will make a helper suitable for him.' " The fact that God created male and female means that home is written into the nature of man and woman. Jesus said, "The two will become one flesh." Sex is to be part of marriage—for fulfillment, for communication, for propagation and for enjoyment. If God is in your marriage, sex is communication at one of the deepest levels of your being.

The Bible warns against intermarriage on religious grounds. We read in 2 Corinthians 6:14, "Do not be mismated with unbelievers." In other words, the person who has committed his life to Jesus Christ is forbidden to marry an unbeliever. Regarding the marriage of a widow, the Apostle Paul says that she is at liberty to be married to whom she will, "only in the Lord." The New English Bible translates it, "Provided the marriage is within the Lord's fellowship."

Any union that does not last until death falls short of God's purpose. God intended that marriage be for life.

Penetrating analyses are being made as to the reasons for the breakdown of the home. The Bible has regulations concerning marriage, and if these regulations are followed carefully in every home, there will be little divorce, and unhappiness in the home will be greatly diminished. But there will not be any perfect marriage. You will never be married to a perfect man or a perfect woman. There is no such person.

The basic reason for unhappiness in our homes is that we have departed from God's Word. We have refused to acknowledge God's plan. As a result, many of our homes are in serious trouble. What is needed is a return to the biblical principles of marriage. We have taken the advice of so-called experts instead of the advice of God. We turn on the television, and someone who has been married five times is giving advice on how to keep marriages together. No wonder we are in trouble!

What does the Bible say? First, the Bible teaches about the duty of the husband. The husband is to love his wife: "Let every one of you in particular so love his wife even as himself." The husband is to love his wife "as Christ also loved the church, and gave himself for it." The Bible says, "Husbands, love your wives, and do not be harsh with them." That word "harsh"

> "THE BASIC REASON FOR UNHAPPINESS IN OUR HOMES IS THAT WE HAVE DEPARTED FROM GOD'S WORD. WE HAVE REFUSED TO ACKNOWLEDGE GOD'S PLAN."

includes cutting remarks. The husband should never criticize his wife and hold her up to ridicule. That is not God's way.

Not only is the husband to love his wife but, second, the husband is primarily to provide for his wife. Notice I said "primarily." Scripture lays on the man the primary responsibility to provide the support for the family: "But if any provide not for his own, and specially for those of his own house, he hath denied the faith, and is worse than an infidel."

In our society some women have to work. In thousands of cases there is no other way. But I believe that if it is at all possible, the mother ought to be home while the children are young. I don't remember coming home, as a boy, when my mother wasn't there. And I think that rarely did our children come home that my wife wasn't there.

I know that some women have

to work. But there are a lot of people who feel that the wife should have a career, even while the children are growing up. Unless you have to work, give your time to your children.

Third, the husband is to be faithful to his wife. Infidelity is one of the few sins for which God demands the death penalty in the Old Testament. God demanded the death penalty in the Old Testament because of adultery.

Fourth, the husband is to give his wife his confidence. She is not a plaything. She is not an ornament. She is a helpmate in all features of his life. He is to confide in her, seek her advice and her counsel.

Fifth, the husband is to lead in the biblical instruction and prayer in the home. Christian husbands and wives are the simplest form of the local church. The Lord said, "Where two or three are gathered together in my name, there am I in the midst." Where two are gathered, just you and your wife, God is in the midst. It is a wonderful thing for the children to see the father leading devotions. "Train up a child in the way he should go: and when he is old, he will not depart from it." If anyone thinks he can train up a child in the way he ought to go and not walk that way himself, he will be disillusioned. Fathers must set the example in prayer, in Bible reading, in churchgoing, in honesty, in integrity. Children will learn far more by watching than by just listening.

Young men who are thinking about marrying should ask themselves these questions about the woman they are dating: "Can I be all this to her? Am I willing to give her myself and not just things instead of me? Am I willing to cover

her faults in love with God's help? Am I willing to be patient, to cherish her as God would have me to do? If not, then don't marry her. And the same is true for young women.

What is the wife's responsibility? "Wives, submit yourselves unto your own husbands, as unto the Lord." That verse has been a stumbling block to many people. The Greek word for "submit" is one which means to yield to one another in the Lord, and this adjustment can be thrilling. We come from different backgrounds, different homes, different parents, different professions, different situations, different cultures - all kinds of differences. And yet we are to adjust to one another.

Seldom has a marriage developed into an individual relationship smoothly and without crises. Accept some differences. Don't be surprised when they come. Crises will come. Troubles will come. Difficulties and differences of opinion will come.

The wife is also to love her husband: "Love [your] husbands." And the wife is to be primarily responsible for keeping the home. There needs to be communication, understanding, mutual help. The husband and wife are equal in mind, in conscience, in position, in privilege.

The first element in a Christian marriage – in a happy Christian home – is that the principle of love must be practiced. The Bible says, "And Isaac . . . took Rebekah, and she became his wife; and he loved her." Do you love your husband? Do you love your wife? Do you tell each other that? You ought to tell each other many times a day.

Psychologists have found that touch means so much. Just touching, hugging, holding hands. How long has it been since you walked down the street holding hands with your wife? You say, "My goodness, she's gray-headed; she's old, and I'm old." I knew a couple in their nineties who walked down the street every day holding hands. What a wonderful sight it was!

"So ought men to love their wives as their own bodies." "Husbands, love your wives, and be not bitter against them." We are to love and care for them.

Does your home belong to Christ? Your house needs to be set in order. You need to give yourself to Christ so that you can be the right kind of husband or wife or child.

What about the children? The word "discipline" means to instruct. Too often the job of teaching is left to the schoolteacher, or the social worker, or the youth club leader. Whether or not we like it, life is filled with certain rules. If a child is to survive, he must know the rules of safety. If he is to be healthy, he must know the rules of health. If he is to drive a car, he must know the rules of the road. If he is to become a ball player, he must learn the rules of the game.

And, contrary to popular thinking, children appreciate rules. Children respect discipline. They want to be guided. It gives them a sense of belonging, a sense of security. By discipline I don't mean constant scolding or nagging or physical violence. Children do need the guidance of their parents, and we guide them more by the example we set than by any other way. We need to be firm and sane and fair and consistent – and, above all, we need to discipline in a spirit of love.

How many of us feel like fail-ures in our home and in our relationship with the family? Do you? You can surrender your heart to

///

"HOW MANY OF US FEEL LIKE FAILURES IN OUR HOME AND IN OUR RELATIONSHIP WITH THE FAMILY? DO YOU?"

///

Christ, and he will forgive you of all of those sins and all those failures. He will change you and give you a new power and a new strength to go in a new direction, to live a new life and to be the right kind of husband and father or wife and mother or child, in the home and in the community and in the church. There is salvation for each of us if we put our trust in Christ.

Joshua said, "Choose you this day whom [you] will serve; . . . but as for me and my house, we will serve the Lord." Every one of us must choose for or against Christ. We cannot be neutral.

You need to surrender to him and say, "Lord, I want You to be not only my Savior but my Lord. I want You to be first. I want You to take control of me. I'm willing to surrender to You totally, without reservation. I'm ready to start reading the Bible and to start prayers in my home." It will be difficult the first time to take your wife's hand and say, "Let's have prayer together." But it will be worth it a thousand times.

Receive Christ into your heart—maybe in a new way, maybe for the first time. Whatever it is, God knows your heart.

First, you need to repent of your sins: "Repent: for the kingdom of heaven is at hand." That word "repent" means that you are willing to change your mind and change the direction of your life – change your way of living, change your habits. You may not be able to do it, but God will help you if you are willing. That's repentance.

Second, you need to come to the cross where Christ shed his blood and say, "I believe, I commit, I surrender totally to Christ for my forgiveness and for my salvation. I know that only his blood can wash away all my sins."

Third, you need to be willing to follow him and obey him and serve him.

Genesis 2:18, NIV. (2) Matthew 19:5, NIV. (3) 2 Corinthians 6:14, RSV. (4) 1 Corinthians 7:39, RSV. (5) 1 Corinthians 7:39, NEB. (6) Ephesians 5:33, KJV. (7) Ephesians 5:25, KJV. (8) Colossians 3:19, RSV. (9) 1 Timothy 5:8, KJV. (10) Leviticus 20:10. (11) Matthew 18:20, KJV. (12) Proverbs 22:6, KJV. (13) Ephesians 5:22, KJV. (14) Titus 2:4, KJV. (15) Titus 2:5. (16) Genesis 24:67, KJV. (17) Ephesians 5:28, KJV. (18) Colossians 3:19, KJV. (19) Joshua 24:15, KJV. (20) Matthew 4:17, KJV.

—William Franklin "Billy" Graham, Jr. (1918-2014) was an American Christian evangelist. He held large indoor and outdoor rallies, and his sermons were broadcast on radio and television. As of 2008, Graham's estimated lifetime audience, including radio and television broadcasts, topped 2.2 billion. Graham was on Gallup's List of Most Admired Man and Woman 55 times since 1955, more than any other individual in the world.

Reprinted by permission: Billy Graham Evangelistic Association

LESSON 2

GROWING IN THE LIKENESS OF CHRIST

MAIN PRINCIPLE

We need to grow in the likeness of Christ and take this likeness into our marriage. Scripture shows us how to become the kind of spouse God wants us to be. The fruit of the Spirit can be manifested in us, enhancing our marriage.

FRUIT OF THE SPIRIT — IN MARRIAGE

Galatians 5:22-23

1. If we walk in the Spirit and desire to be like Him, we will have the fruit of the Spirit, which can greatly benefit our marriage.

   a. **Love**—"divine love; a strong ardent, tender, compassionate devotion to the well-being" of our spouse; unconditional (agape) love for our spouse.

   b. **Joy**—"the emotional excitement, gladness, delight over blessings received or expected for ourself" or our mate.

   c. **Peace**—"the state of quietness, rest, repose, harmony, order and serenity in the midst of turmoil, strife and temptations."

   d. **Longsuffering**—"patient endurance; to bear long with the frailties, offenses, injuries and provocations of of others, without murmuring, repining (complaining) or resentment."

   e. **Gentleness**—"a disposition to be gentle, soft-spoken, kind, even-tempered, cultured and refined in character and conduct."

   f. **Goodness**—"the state of being good, kind, virtuous, benevolent, generous and God like in life and conduct."

   g. **Faith**—"the living, divinely-implanted, acquired, and created principle of inward and wholehearted confidence, assurance, trust and reliance in God and all that He says."

   h. **Meekness**—"the disposition to be gentle, kind, indulgent, even balanced in tempers and passions, and patient in suffering injuries without a feeling of revenge."

   i. **Temperance**—"self control; a moderation in the indulgence of the appetites and passions." A curbing of the fleshly impulses.

2. There is no one more attractive than a person whose life manifests the fruit of the Spirit.

The quoted portions of this article come from Finis Jennings Dake, *Dakes Annoted Reference Bible* (Larenceville, Georgia, Dake Bible Sales, Inc, 1963), p. 206, column 1, note c. Used by permission.

FRUIT OF THE SPIRIT — IN MARRIAGE

Galatians 5:22-23

CALLED TO BE CHRIST-LIKE

by David Wilkerson

Recently, a dear Christian woman told me, "I'm learning my purpose in life through a class I'm taking." She was finishing an eight-week course meant to help people discover their calling. She said everyone in the class was anxious to find their purpose.

I heard a pastor on the radio advertising something similar. He offered to help listeners discover their spiritual gifts. If you would request his questionnaire, fill it out and send it in, his staff would evaluate your particular gifts. Then they would tell you how to find your place in the body of Christ.

A frustrated ministry couple wrote to me, "We've been looking for ways to fulfill God's calling in our lives. But we've run into all kinds of hindrances. We're so discouraged, at times we feel like giving up." Maybe this couple will turn to the resources these others are using. I'm sure such tools are helpful to some degree. The Bible says God gives gifts to his people, and I believe there are special callings.

Yet I'm convinced by Scripture there is only one core purpose for all believers. Our specific callings are gathered up in this single purpose, and every gift springs from it. And if we miss this purpose, all our desires and pursuits will be in vain.

Jesus sums up our core purpose in John 15:16: "Ye have not chosen me, but I have chosen you, and ordained you that he should go and bring forth fruit." Our purpose is simply this: we are all called and chosen to bear fruit.

WHAT IS THE FRUIT WE ARE CALLED TO BEAR?

Many sincere Christians think bearing fruit means simply to bring souls to Christ. But to bear fruit means something much larger even than soul-winning.

The fruit Jesus is talking about is Christ-likeness. Simply put, bearing fruit means reflecting the likeness of Jesus. And the phrase "much fruit" means "the ever-increasing likeness of Christ."

Growing more and more into Jesus' likeness is our core purpose in life. It has to be central to all our activities, our life-style, our relationships. Indeed, all our gifts and callings—our work, ministry and witness—must flow out of this core purpose.

If I am not Christ-like at heart—if I'm not becoming noticeably more like him—I have totally missed God's purpose for my life. It doesn't matter what I accomplish for his kingdom. If I miss this one purpose, I have lived, preached and striven in vain.

You see, God's purpose for me can't be fulfilled by what I do for Christ. It can't be measured by anything I achieve, even if I heal the sick or cast out demons. No. God's purpose is fulfilled in me only by what I am becoming in him. Christ-likeness isn't about what I do for the Lord, but about how I'm being transformed into his likeness.

> "YE KNOW HIM; FOR HE DWELLETH WITH YOU, AND SHALL BE IN YOU…. HE SHALL TEACH YOU ALL THINGS" (John 14:17, 26).

In the disciples' minds, the temple in Jerusalem was a great, godly work, a magnificent accomplishment. They took Jesus on a tour to show him the grandeur of the structures, the huge crowds who gathered daily, all the religious activities that took place there. They thought Christ would be just as impressed with it as they were.

Instead, Jesus threw a wet blanket on their enthusiasm. He told them, in essence, "This is all coming down. Not one stone here will remain. All these crowds are going to scatter, and even the shepherds will flee. Everything here that impresses you—everything that looks religious—is going to be rejected. And it will happen because *this is not Christ-revealing*. It is man-centered, and it's man-revealing."

The fact is, the disciples had been focusing on the wrong temple. They had their eyes on this man-made temple. Their focus was on the religious activity. And they were being impressed by the wrong things. What happened there did not represent the Father. The temple had become a den of thieves and money-changers. The prophets and priests were out for themselves. They even robbed and abused their own parents. The temple was not about Christ's purposes at all.

In short, Jesus refocused the disciples' attention on the spiritual temple. As Paul would later write to the church, "Don't you know your body is the temple of the Lord?"

I believe that many Christians today are like the disciples. We're impressed by huge church edifices, by multitudes who stream in on Sunday, by the uniqueness of the worship, by multiple programs and ministries. But Jesus' message to us is clear: we are not to focus on buildings of stone and metal, on forms of worship or on how church is conducted. Those things will only distract us. Instead, our focus should be on our spiritual temple.

The fact is, the Holy Spirit is in his temple at all times. He abides in our bodies. And he is prepared at any moment to bring us into his purpose. That means we have to have our spiritual house in order.

There are times we are called to speak righteous judgment. Scripture calls every Christian to expose false doctrines and false prophets. Ministers especially are to denounce in God's house that which is unlike Christ.

But Peter says judgment begins in the house of God. And "house" doesn't mean just the church, but our human temple as well. I am to judge myself—to look at the condition of my own temple—before I'm able to judge anything I see in the church.

Jesus says, "Every branch in me that beareth not fruit he taketh away…If a man abide not in me, he is cast forth as a branch, and is withered; and men gather them, and cast them into the fire, and they are burned" (John 15:2, 6). Whatever in the church isn't a reflection of Christ—whatever is corrupt or false, or doesn't bring his people into his likeness—will be dealt with. Jesus will cast it out. And he'll cause that ministry and its wicked perpetrators to wither. He'll eventually expose it, bankrupt it and shut it down.

I'm convinced that if any Christian living today could have walked through the temple in Jesus' time, he would have been grieved by what he saw. Priests pocketing money on the side, greed and corruption, money madness—all of it would be shocking. That Christian would wonder, "How long will the Lord endure such foolishness in his house?"

Yet, the truth is, the condition of the temple would have been nothing for us to worry about. Jesus did cast out the wickedness there. He brought in a cord and whip and cleansed his Father's house. And he brought down all the corrupt ministries that were operating in it.

Today, we serve the same temple-cleansing Christ. And he's faithful to cast out all corruption in his church, in his time and his way. If he chose, he could bring down every false prophet overnight. Therefore, we're to trust him to take care of his church. Our part is to make sure that no worldliness creeps into our own human temple.

PAUL SAYS, "WE ARE CALLED ACCORDING TO HIS PURPOSE."

"We know that all things work together for good to them that love God, to them who are called according to his purpose" (Romans 8:28). Paul's message here is simple. "All things ought to be working out for good in the lives of those who love God and walk in his ways."

This truth causes me to wonder: why is there so much discouragement and distress among Christians? Why are so many pastors worn out, weary and leaving the ministry in droves around the world? Why is there such awful competition between ministries?

I see churches everywhere mired in materialism and deep in debt. And all the while, the people beg for answers in their lives. I ask you, how could this be the abundant life Paul says we're supposed to enjoy? It doesn't look anything like a good life. Honestly it looks like a life of misery. Just go into any Christian bookstore and read the titles on the shelves. Most are self-help books on how to overcome loneliness, how to survive depression, how to find fulfillment. Why is this?

It's because we've got it all wrong. We aren't called to be successes, to be free of all trouble, to be special, to "make it." No, we're missing the one calling, the one focus, that's meant to be central to our lives: to become fruitful in the likeness of Christ.

> "WE KNOW THAT ALL THINGS WORK TOGETHER FOR GOOD TO THEM THAT LOVE GOD, TO THEM WHO ARE THE CALLED ACCORDING TO HIS PURPOSE" (Romans 8:28).

When I was twenty-nine years old, an older, well-known evangelist asked me to lunch. He advised me, "If you don't make it by the time you're fifty, you'll never make it. I have five more years, and after that my chances for success are gone. So, I'm going to start a national TV program."

I thought to myself, "Make it? This doesn't sound like the language of Christ's calling." Soon after that, God put this man on the shelf. He was lost in oblivion, all his dream shattered. Sadly, I hear tales like his in my travels these days. Several ministers have told me, "I'm going to build a mega-church."

A man who once attended our church told me, "I get so angry when I see everyone else making it big time, while I have so many financial needs. It's my turn now. I'm going to do whatever it takes." The last I heard of that man, the law was after him.

The truth is, many of us are called to be ordinary Christians. Yet we put such pressure on ourselves to keep up with the competitive spirit in the world today. We drive our children to be doctors, lawyers, prominent business people, even "successful" ministers. But we don't have to produce anything to find our purpose in life. We don't have to erect buildings, write books or draw crowds. Paul says we are predestined to be conformed to the likeness of Christ, and that is our one purpose: "For whom he did foreknow, he also did predestinate to be conformed to the image of his Son, that he might be the firstborn among many brethren" (Romans 8:29).

Jesus was totally given to the Father, and that was everything to him. He stated, "I don't do or say anything except what my Father tells me." Paul is telling us that every believer is to follow the same pattern and direction, to have the same core interest: "I am here for my Lord."

So, do you want to bear the "much fruit" that springs forth from becoming more like Christ? I asked myself that question as I prepared this message. And the Spirit whispered to me. "David, you have to be willing to look at how you deal with others."

Simply put, bearing fruit comes down to how we treat people. We fulfill our life's purpose only as we begin to love others as Christ has loved us. And we grow more Christ-like as our love for others increases. Jesus said, "As the Father hath loved me, so have I loved you: continue ye in my love" (John 15:9). His command is clear and simple. "Go and love others. Give to others the unconditional love I have shown you."

The Spirit impressed on me three areas where Christ's unconditional love must begin:

1. THIS LOVE HAS TO BEGIN IN OUR HOMES.

Jesus' command has to do with how I treat my spouse and children. For single people, it involves how you treat roommates, fellow Christians, the people closest to you.

This truth was at the core of Malachi's prophecy to Israel. God said to the priests of that day, "This ye have done again, covering the altar of the Lord with tears, with weeping, and with crying out, insomuch that he regardeth not the offering any more, or receiveth it with good will at your hand" (Malachi 2:13). God was saying, "I no longer accept your offering or your worship. I won't receive anything you bring."

Why didn't God accept these men's ministry any longer? "Because the Lord hath been witness between thee and the wife of thy youth, against whom thou hast dealt treacherously…Take heed" (2:14-15). It all had to do with their marriages.

There's no getting around it. If I am to become the man and minister God has called me to be, then my wife must be able to say honestly before heaven, hell and all the world, "My husband loves me with the love of Christ. He makes mistakes, but he's growing more patient and understanding with me. He's becoming more tender and caring. And he prays with me. He isn't a phony. He is what he preaches."

Now, I help pastor what would be called a mega-church. I conduct ministers' conferences around the world, preaching to thousands at a time. I founded Teen Challenge, a Christian rehabilitation ministry for alcoholics and drug addicts, which now has 500 centers worldwide. I've written some twenty books, helped establish a Bible school, set up a home for abandoned mothers and their children. I've had honors heaped on me.

But if this isn't my wife's testimony—if she has a secret pain in her heart, thinking, "My husband isn't the man of God he pretends to be"—then everything in my life is in vain. All my works—the preaching, the accomplishments, the charitable giving, the many travels—amount to nothing. I am a withering, useless branch that doesn't bear the fruit of Christ-likeness. Jesus will cause others to see the death in me, and I'll be worth little to his kingdom.

You can evangelize all you want, witnessing and passing out tracts. You can go to church week after week and sing praises to God. But what does your spouse have to say about you? What kind of life do you lead in your home?

A middle-aged pastor and his wife came to me brokenhearted and weeping. The minister told me through tears, "Brother Dave, I have sinned against God and my wife. I've committed adultery." He shook with godly sorrow as he confessed his sin to me. Then his wife turned to me and said softly, "I've forgiven him. His repentance is real to me. I know he isn't that kind of man. I'm confident the Lord will restore us."

I was privileged to witness the beginnings of a beautiful healing. We can never make up for our past failures. But when there is true repentance, God promises to restore all that the cankerworm has destroyed.

Yet, the treachery that Malachi describes isn't just about adultery or fornication. It includes everything that can be called un-Christ-like, such as mean-spiritedness, bitterness and dishonesty. These kinds of treacheries also void our lifetime accomplishments. God says to all who commit them, "I will not accept your works, your worship or anything you bring to me. I have a controversy with you."

I deeply wish every couple who enjoys a Christ-centered marriage would rise up and tell the truth: "It isn't easy." Marriage is a day-by-day effort, in the same way the Christian life is. Like the way of the Cross,

---

"THAT THE LOVE WHEREWITH THOU HAST LOVED ME MAY BE IN THEM, AND I IN THEM" (John 17-26).

it means giving up your rights daily. Of course, Satan knows your heart is set on becoming more Christ-like in your home, so he's constantly going to bring about trials.

In short, there is no other school as difficult and intense as the school of marriage. And you never graduate. God is making it clear to us: Our life with our loved ones is the pinnacle, the very summit, of all our testings. If we get it wrong here, we'll have it wrong everywhere else in our life.

2. CHRIST-LIKENESS ALSO HAS TO DO WITH HOW I TREAT THOSE OUTSIDE MY FAMILY.

To be Christ-like is to acknowledge Jesus in others. In my travels, I meet many precious men and women whom I know are given wholly to the Lord. The moment I meet them, my heart leaps. Even though we've never met before, I have a witness from the Holy Spirit that they're full of Christ.

I can still see some of their faces: pastors, bishops, poor street evangelists. And the moment I met them, I realized without a word being spoken, "This man has been with Jesus. This woman is satisfied in Christ." In greeting them, I always say the one thing I would want others to say of me: "Brother, sister, I see Jesus in you." I don't mean it as flattery; it is the witness of the Holy Spirit.

We know that Christ-likeness means loving others as he loves us. Yet it also means loving our enemies—those who hate us, who despitefully use us, who aren't capable of loving us. And we're to do this expecting nothing in return. Of course, loving this way is impossible, in human terms. There aren't any how-to books, any set of principles, or any amount of human intelligence to show us how to love our enemies as Christ loves us. Yet we're commanded to do it. And we're to do it with ever-increasing purpose. According to Jesus, that's the fruit we are to bear.

So, how do we do it? How do I love the Muslim who spat in my face a block away from our church? How do I love the people who run internet websites calling me a false prophet? How do I love homosexuals who parade down Fifth Avenue carrying signs declaring, "Jesus Was Gay"? How do I truly love them in Christ? I don't even know how to love other Christians in my own ability.

Very simply, it has to be the work of the Holy Spirit. As Jesus prayed to the Father, "That the love wherewith thou hast loved me may be in them, and I in them (John 17:26). Christ asks the Father to put his love in us. And he promises that the Holy Spirit will show us how to live out that love.

"Howbeit when he, the Spirit of truth, is come, he will guide you into all truth: for he shall not speak of himself; but whatsoever he shall hear, that shall he speak: and he will shew you things to come. He shall glorify me: for he shall receive of mine, and shall shew it unto you… He shall take of mine, and shall shew it unto you" (John 16:13-15).

Do you hear what Jesus is saying here? The Holy Ghost will faithfully gather up all the ways Christ loved others and "show it to you." Indeed, the Spirit delights in showing us more of Jesus. It's the reason he dwells in our bodily temples: to teach Christ to us. "Ye know him; for he dwelleth with you, and shall be in you… He shall teach you all things" (John 14:17, 26).

3. FINALLY, AN UN-CHRIST-LIKE DIVISION IN THE CHURCH HAS ROBBED IT OF POWER AND INFLUENCE IN EVERY NATION.

In apostolic times, the church was so filled with Christ's authority, it caused kings and rulers to tremble. Paul and his young pastors and evangelists preached fearlessly. They filled entire cities and nations with the message of Jesus. Here was a church known for its Christ-likeness, its power to affect heaven and earth.

Yet today, much of the church has been left a weak, feeble institution, with little of Christ's authority. It is being mocked and ridiculed the world over. As I travel from nation to nation, I can see why. I often find the church in a sad condition, marked by narrow denominationalism. Each group claims to be of Christ and to preach a biblical gospel. Yet in some cases, these groups can't even sit down at a table together.

Happily, in many nations, Christian leaders cross denominational lines to help bring about our conferences. But a great divide often still exists between cultures and races. Certain groups are looked down upon

and aren't even invited to the meetings. Also, new religious movements are springing up everywhere, with true revival taking place. But some of these have become exclusive, claiming they alone have the truth.

Finally, there is another kind of division in the church that is absolutely un-Christ-like. It is the chasm between the large and the small: those who are doing big things in the Lord's name, versus those who are called to smaller works.

God has a rebuke for this kind of division: "Who hath despised the day of small things?" (Zechariah 4:10). This was his word to the Israelites who despised the temple foundation laid by Zerubbabel. They looked down on the new work because it wasn't as spectacular as Solomon's temple.

Likewise today, many pastors' conferences are emphasizing mega-church growth. Ministers from small churches are being told, in so many words, "Attend this mega-church pastor's seminar, and you'll find the keys to success. You'll eventually have a church as big as his." Yet this only causes pastors to become more discouraged. They end up convinced, "I'm not doing anything significant for God. He just isn't using me."

I honestly would love to attend a ministers' conference where all the speakers were pastors from small or average-size churches. I don't have any desire to hear about how to build a large church or raise a huge budget. I would rather hear twenty or thirty small-church pastors speak about what God is saying to them, about the revelation of Christ they're receiving.

Maybe you're thinking, "I'm one of those little people. The things I do in God's kingdom are so small. I'm not involved in anything important for the Lord." That is not the case. Let me tell you how I believe God sees this whole matter.

The most useful people in the church of Jesus Christ are those who have eyes to see and ears to hear. Yes, some people are doing great things that are seen and heard by many. But some of those ministers don't have eyes to see the needs of hurting people. They are project-oriented rather than need-oriented.

The simple fact is, the Christ who lives in me is not blind or deaf. And his Word says, "Whoso hath this world's goods, and seeth his brother have need, and shutteth up his bowels of compassion from him, how dwelleth the love of God in him?" (1 John 3:17). Jesus sees all the needs and hurts around me. He hears the groanings and cries of the distressed and bound. And if I am to be more like him, then I need his eyes to see the same things.

This is the love of Christ: to hear the distressing cry of the fatherless, the child of the ghetto…the lonely, muffled cry of the homosexual who's sick of his sin, drowning his torment in alcohol…the agonized cries of the hungry, the poor, the imprisoned. Being like Christ is having such "eyes to see and ears to hear."

Oh, Lord, give me a listening ear. Help me to quit telling people how much I know. Instead, help me to hear what you're saying to those who have no public voice. Help me to be a student at the feet of unknown pastors and servants in the body who are truly bearing much fruit. Let me hear what you're saying through them. And let me love others not in word only, but in deed and in truth.

—David Wilkerson died in 2011. He was the founding pastor of Times Square Church in New York City. There he ministered to gang members and drug addicts. In 1971, he founded World Challenge, Inc., which supports missionaries and outreaches throughout the world.

Reprinted by permission: World Challenge, Inc., PO Box 260, Lindale, TX 75771. http://worldchallenge.org

A NEW HEART

by U.S. Grant

The scriptures tell us some things about the heart that are not very flattering.

Jesus taught that "…out of the heart proceed evil thoughts, murders, adulteries, fornications, thefts, false witness, blasphemies" (Matt. 15:19). One could cut off a thief's hand or cut out a liar's tongue (Matt 5:30), but the inclination to thievery and false witness would still be in the heart.

Jesus also taught that to hate a person in one's heart is tantamount to murder (Matt. 5:22) and that adultery and/or fornication can be an act of the heart even if it is not overt (Matt. 5:28).

The record in Mark says much more. Adding to Matthew's account, and still quoting Jesus, he says that out of the heart proceed "Thefts, covetousness, wickedness, deceit, lasciviousness (shameless conduct, wantonness, unmanageable, loose morals), an evil eye, blasphemy, pride, foolishness" (Mk. 7:22).

Our speech also is a revelation of what is in the heart, "…for out of the abundance of the heart the mouth speaketh" (Matt. 12:34). "A good man out of the good treasure of the heart bringeth forth good things: and an evil man out of the evil treasure bringeth forth evil things" (Matt. 12:35).

The heart can be hardened against the truth of the Gospel. "…Today, after so long a time; as it is said, Today if ye will hear his voice, harden not your hearts" (Heb. 4:7).

What kind of a heart is it that, according to the prophet Ezekiel, needs to be removed and replaced by a different heart? It is a stony heart (Ezek. 36:26). The stony heart is a froward heart—crooked or perverse. The psalmist writes, "A froward heart shall depart from me…" (Psa. 101:4). Proverbs declares it is, "An heart that deviseth wicked imaginations…" (Prov. 6:18). Jeremiah says it is a "…revolting and a rebellious heart…" (Jer. 5:23). He also declares that, "The heart is deceitful above all things, and desperately wicked: who can know it?" (Jer. 17:9).

The old heart is just no good. It cannot be repaired. It is like Humpty Dumpty that sat on a wall and had a great fall: all the king's horses and all the king's men couldn't put Humpty Dumpty together again.

Jesus taught that a corrupt tree—no matter how beautiful the foliage—cannot bring forth good fruit (Matt. 7:18). That one does not put new wine in old wineskins. The old wineskins cannot change

(Mk. 2:21,22). One can wash the outside of the cup and platter, but the inside is still unclean-full of extortion and excess (Matt. 23:25). He likened the Pharisees to "…whited sepulchers, which indeed appear beautiful outward, but are within full of dead men's bones, and of all uncleanness" (Matt. 23:27).

Dr. Adam Clarke, the Methodist commentator, in explaining Ezekiel 36:26, speaks at some length about God's attitude toward the old heart. "A new heart also will I give you…." The Lord will change the whole of your infected nature, and give you new appetites and new passions. The heart is generally understood to mean all the affections and passions.

"…And a new spirit will I put within you…." God will renew your minds, also enlighten your understanding, correct your judgment and refine your will.

So that you will have a new spirit to actuate your new heart, "…I (God) will take away the stony heart…." That heart is hard, impenetrable and cold; with affections and passions that are unyielding, frozen to good, unaffected by heavenly things, slow to credit the words of God.

The Lord will entirely remove

this heart. It is the opposite to that which He has promised you; and you cannot have the new heart and the old heart at the same time.

—Adapted from Heart Transplant by U.S. Grant.

Rev. U.S. Grant pastored one the Assemblies of God's largest churches for many years in Kansas City, Kansas. Though retired, he is still active in ministry.

Reprinted by permission: Christ for the Nations CFNI, P.O. Box 769000, Dallas, TX 75376-9000, 800-933-2364

LESSON 3

IN THE BEGINNING GOD CREATED

MAIN PRINCIPLE

God created male and female. Each is unique, created to be different, but created for each other. God meant for man and wife to live side by side in complementary roles.

UNDIVIDED: GOD'S PLAN FOR COUPLES IN THE MINISTRY

by Sam and Cheri Benson

Independence is the cry of our world today. Men and women are possessed with the idea of "making it on their own." Striving to prove their self-sufficiency, their lifestyles exemplify a need for no one. Self-esteem by the world's standard is measured by how well a person does alone.

Covering our eyes and pretending not to notice, we have allowed this spirit of the world to creep into the church. Today's heart-cry for unity in the body of Christ is necessary because for years God's people have functioned independently of one another. Even more alarming is the realization that this deception didn't begin with laity and move toward the leadership. The worldly spirit of independence infiltrated leadership and thus affected laity. In the name of ministry many marriages have been sacrificed and families destroyed. Every imaginable excuse has been utilized, yet the truth remains: We cannot bring healing, wholeness and unity to the body of Christ while those in the ministry are sick, incomplete and divided.

The prophet Malachi makes strong statements concerning those in the ministry when he says, "For the lips of a priest should keep knowledge, and people should seek the law from his mouth; for he is the messenger of the Lord of hosts. But you have departed from the way; you have caused many to stumble at the law; you have corrupted the covenant of Levi" (Malachi 2:7-8; NKJV).

Then Malachi goes on to declare that the greatest corruption the ministry would know is the corruption that would take place between the husbands and wives in the ministry. Verses 13-15 say, "And this is the second thing you do: You cover the altar of the Lord with tears, with weeping and crying; so He does not regard the offering anymore, nor receive it with good will from your hands. Yet you say, 'For what reason?' Because the Lord has been witness between you and the wife of your youth, with whom you have dealt treacherously; yet she is your companion and your wife by covenant. But did he not make them one, having a remnant of the Spirit? And why one? He seeks godly offspring. Therefore take heed to your spirit, and let none deal treacherously with the wife of his youth."

In the ministry today, many marriages are falling to demise and disgrace because we have failed to consider one another as companions by covenant. God has established that we walk with one another in a one-flesh covenant that provides protection and power through unity.

Throughout the Genesis account of Creation, we continually find God's assessment of His creative work with the words, "And God saw it was good," or, "God saw it was very good." Yet Genesis 2:18 reads, "It is not good that man should be alone." God wanted His man to be able to enjoy protection and share life and power through a one-flesh covenant. God declared, "It is not good that a man's strength should be spread out like this." So God created a "helpmate." The New King James Bible defines "helpmate" as a helper comparable to him; a partner who would fit into God's plans. But the literal Hebrew translation is: "I will make someone to help Adam like he is helping me."

Ministry is the result of marriage as God intended it to be. Let's investigate God's intentions for man and woman to understand how we are to function as co-rulers in His kingdom.

Marriage is to be a harmonious union where people grow together and live their lives in peace, love and dominion. God said concerning mankind, "Let them have dominion." Notice He did not say "Let him." As we understand the word "dominion," it means complete authority over all the earth; over everything that moves on the earth. Literally, the word "dominion" means to have the right and power to govern and control. God intended that man and woman together live their lives in love, peace and dominion in order that God's purpose be fulfilled in the earth.

What's necessary for this unity to mature and develop? Here are four suggestions:

1. Pray together.
2. Share the Word of God together.
3. Listen to God together.
4. Do God's will together.

It's not enough for each individual to mature in the Lord. The marriage must mature in the Lord also. Ephesians 4:16 says we grow to full maturity when each part is working properly, building itself up in love. When two spiritually mature people operate in unity, they complement one another to the degree that everything they do pleases God and it produces protection for their marriage and power in their ministries.

PROTECTION THROUGH UNITY

No one is more aware of the fatalities occurring among ministers today than ministers themselves. All too frequently we hear reports of men and women greatly used of God who have been trapped in the snare of the enemy, falling into moral sin and losing their opportunity for effective ministry. It seems incomprehensible that such things could happen. Yet the situation repeats itself time and time again.

In 18 years of ministry, we have yet to hear of a ministry fatality where the marriage was based on the one-flesh covenant. It is impossible for Satan to get a foothold in a ministry protected through unity.

POWER THROUGH UNITY

When men and women operate and function in marriage as God intends, then the marriage enjoys godly leadership, discernment and intercession. As a ministry couple walks in unity, they experience the power of agreement. Jesus said in Matthew 18:19, "Again I say to you that if two of you agree on earth touching anything that they ask, will be done for them by my Father which is in heaven." Jesus literally provides the open door to a future ministry filled with excitement and satisfaction. And not only does the power of agreement open the doors to future ministry, it also releases our lives from the chains of satanic oppression. Because of the power of agreement, there is also the power of multiplied effectiveness. God's Word shares the vital principle: "One chases a thousand, two put 10,000 to flight."

Recently the Lord said to us, "As you minister together, the effectiveness of your ministry will be multiplied 10 times. There will be more decisions for Christ, more healings, more signs and more wonders as you move together." We have literally experienced untold benefits from moving in unity and experiencing the power of agreement and multiplied effectiveness.

As your marriage grows stronger day by day in the bond of unity because it is founded on the Word of God and rooted and grounded in the love of God, you will experience security in the protection of your marriage and power in the performance of your ministry. The time has come for the leaders of the church to cast off the spirit of the world and resist the deception that has crept into the body of Christ. God is calling for His ministers to rise up in the fullness of His provision, and out of their marriage covenant they should minister health, wholeness, unity and love to the body of Christ.

—Cheri and Sam Benson have served as Senior Pastors of Destiny Christian Center in Puyallup WA. "Building your family, building your future" is the theme of their teaching and vision. Sam and Cheri are dedicated to the empowerment of each individual believer and the destiny of the body of Christ.

Cheri, a gifted teacher of God's Word, frequently speaks at conferences, seminars and church events.

GUESS WHAT...GOD KNOWS BEST

by Glenn T. Stanton

Scientific research vindicates the Creator's idea of the family.

Olivia Cobb will be a junior at a state college in the Pacific Northwest when she returns to school this fall. As a Christian with a sociology major, she likes the intellectual challenge of having to defend her beliefs in a secular arena.

Last spring, one of her required courses was "SOC-104: Sociology of the American Family." She looked forward to taking the class, since her own family is so important to her. Raised with four brothers and sisters in a Christian home, Olivia believes her parents gave her a wonderful start in life.

Olivia* soon discovered that her professor, a recognized family scholar and author, also held some definite views on the value of family. Her professor announced early in the semester that she was a social progressive who would quickly challenge any "traditional" thinking from her students. Olivia pondered that statement for a while.

One day, the professor opened class by asking, "Should there be a cultural model— a norm—for family life in America?"

Much of the class looked puzzled. To raise a hand was to give an answer that required a value judgment, and everyone in the class knew it. One student tested the waters by declaring that "love" should be the one necessary ingredient for a good family. Others nodded in agreement, and the professor looked satisfied.

Olivia, knowing that a good family is a bit more complex, decided to raise her hand. "I believe that since families are the building blocks of society, our culture can be only as strong as our families," she said. "In order to have strong families, we should have norms that include, but also go beyond, 'love.' "

The classroom froze for a moment. Didn't she know what she was saying? Olivia wasn't through, however. "For instance, it's best for men and women to save sex for its proper place—marriage," she stated.

A wave of snickers swept across the room, and a fleeting look of condescension could be detected on the professor's face. But Olivia kept boldly to her course.

"In addition, people are better off when they are married," she said. "Therefore, premarital cohabitation and divorce should, once again, be socially stigmatized."

Is this young woman for real? the professor seemed to be thinking. What rock did she climb out from under?

Olivia, gaining confidence, remained undaunted. "All children should be born to or adopted by both a mother and a father who are married and live under the same roof. These should be the norms for family life in our culture."

For a moment, Olivia thought all the air had been sucked out of the room. Many students were shocked, and Olivia saw a few roll their eyes. Then she heard one student whisper, "How could she be so old-fashioned?"

The professor did little to hide her anger. "Thank you for that nice sermon, Miss Cobb, but let me bring you up to date. Check out the newspaper. This is the 20th century, and we've moved beyond that premodern, patriarchal, slave-master, "Leave-It-to-Beaver' mentality of the Judeo-Christian family. In the Dark Ages, it was acceptable to take things on faith, but since then we've had a little development called

* Olivia is a composite character of several students known to the author.

the Enlightenment. If you're going to make such bold claims, you should be able to support them."

Walking up to Olivia's seat, the professor asked, "How would you like to write your term paper defending your thesis? And remember, you have to support your case with recognized scientific data, not with warm religious sentiments."

Some of the students laughed. A few felt badly for Olivia, who tried to recall how God had come into the discussion. But the challenge had been thrown down, and she wasn't about to back away. I know that what God says about family life is true, she thought, but what will the research show? Is His idea of the family empirically defensible by scientific research?

Olivia headed straight to the library after lunch. Searching the library's online card catalog, she found a number of titles on the issue of family well-being. She also sat down at a computer terminal and began surfing the Internet for databases containing social science journal articles. After several hours, Olivia had gathered a wealth of information.

For the next month, Olivia poured herself into the term paper. Once she began writing, she felt confident that she could defend the traditional family using mainstream social science research.

EVIDENCE ON ABSTINENCE

Olivia found strong data revealing that it is indeed wiser to wait until marriage to engage in sexual intercourse. Besides underlining the possibility of becoming one of the 68 million Americans who has contracted an incurable sexually transmitted disease, research showed that sex is more satisfying for those who wait until marriage.

A recent survey of sexuality, which was called the "most authoritative ever" by U.S. News & World Report, provided some definite answers. This survey, conducted jointly by researchers at State University of New York at Stony Brook and the University of Chicago, found that of all sexually active people, "the people who reported being most physically pleased and emotionally satisfied were the married couples."

These researchers found not only that sex is better in marriage, but it is best if you have had only one sexual partner in a lifetime. "[P]hysical and emotional satisfaction started to decline when people had more than one sexual partner," the researchers stated.

MARRIED PEOPLE ARE BETTER OFF

Olivia also established solid support for her assertion that people are better off when married. First, she found that married people have healthier unions than couples who live together. Research from Washington State University revealed, "Cohabiting couples compared to married couples have less healthy relationships."

Second, the data proved married people are generally better off in all measures of well-being. Researchers at UCLA explained that "cohabitors experienced significantly more difficulty in [subsequent] marriages with [issues of] adultery, alcohol, drugs and independence than couples who had not cohabited." In fact, marriages preceded by cohabitation are 50 to 100 percent more likely to break up than those marriages not preceded by cohabitation.

With a national discussion about "wife beating" prompted by the O.J. Simpson trial, Olivia discovered that "wife beating" should more properly be called "girlfriend beating." The reason is, according to the Journal of Marriage and the Family, that "aggression is at least twice as common among cohabitors as it is among married partners."

Olivia also found that married people enjoy better physical and mental health. Dr. Robert Coombs, a biobehavioral scientist at UCLA, conducted a review of more than 130 studies on the relationship between well-being and marital status, concluding that "there is an intimate link between the two."

Coombs found married people had significantly lower rates of alcoholism, suicide, psychiatric care, and higher rates of self-reported happiness.

One of the most respected studies in the field of psychiatry said those in married relationships experienced a lower rate of severe depression than people in any other category. The numbers were as follows (annual rate of major depression per 100):

Married (never divorced).. 1.5
Never married.. 2.4
Divorced once 4.1
Cohabiting.. 5.1
Divorced twice... 5.8

Regarding physical health, researchers at the University of Massachusetts showed that married people experience less disease, morbidity and disability than do those who are divorced or separated. Their explanation: "One of the most consistent observations in health research is that the married enjoy better health than those of other [relational] statuses."

In addition, the U.S. Department of Justice reported in 1994 that men and women are at much greater risk of being assaulted if they are not married. Here were the rates per 1,000 for general aggravated assaults against:

Males:
Married 5.5
Divorced or separated 13.6
Never married... 23.4

Females:
Married 3.1
Divorced or separated 9.4
Never married... 11.9

Clearly, the safest, healthiest place for men and women is marriage.

BEST ENVIRONMENT TO RAISE CHILDREN

What data supported Olivia's claim that children fare better in homes where there are two parents who are married? She looked at more books, government reports and research journal articles. On this topic, she literally found more material than she could read.

The bulk of the material showed that, on average, children do better in all areas when raised by two married parents who live together.

The most authoritative work done in this area is by Dr. Sara McLanahan of Princeton University. In Growing Up With a Single Parent, she explains, "Children who grow up in a household with only one biological parent are worse off, on average, than children who grow up . . . with both of their biological parents, regardless of the parents' race or educational background."

She continues, "Adolescents who have lived apart from one of their parents during some period of childhood are twice as likely to drop out of high school . . . to have a child before age 20, and one-and-a-half times as likely to be idle – out of school and out of work – in their late twenties."

Dr. George Rekers, a practicing clinical psychologist and professor at the University of South Carolina, agreed with McLanahan: "Research has documented that children without fathers more often have lowered academic performance, more cognitive and intellectual deficits, increased adjustment problems, and higher risks for psychosexual development problems."

Dr. David Popenoe, a noted family scholar from Rutgers University, explained that there can be no serious debate over this issue: "I know of few other bodies of data in which the weight of evidence is so decisively on one side of the issue. On the whole, for children, two-parent families are preferable . . . . If our prevailing views on family structure hinged solely on scholarly evidence, the current debate never would have arisen in the first place."

It isn't just having an additional adult in the home that will help solve the problems facing single-parent families. A sociologist at the University of Pennsylvania said: "Most studies show that children in step-families do not do better than children in single-parent families; indeed, many indicate that, on average, children in remarriages do worse."

Olivia was disturbed to find that step-families are the second-fastest growing family structure in America. The fastest is created by out-of-wedlock births.

WHEN DEATH CREATES A SINGLE-PARENT FAMILY

Olivia was intrigued to find that single-parent families created by the death of a spouse have a natural protective mechanism distinguishing them from other single-parent families. Dr. James Egan, a child psychiatrist at Children's Hospital in Washington, D.C., provocatively asserted, "A dead father is a more effective father than a missing father."

This is simply because when a father (or mother) dies, he still maintains a place of authority, influence and moral leadership in the home. Parents who have departed due to death usually leave positive reputations. Their pictures remain on the wall, they are talked about positively, and negative behavior on the part of a child can be corrected with a simple reminder: "Would your dad (or mom) approve of that kind of behavior?"

If the father has abandoned the child or was never identified, the answer to that question is either "Who cares?" or, even worse, "Who?"

COMING TO A CONCLUSION

When Olivia started to write her paper, she thought about all she had learned and wondered why she had been nervous about the assignment. She knew that at creation, God set certain laws into motion with intelligence and intention. This included a norm for family life.

She thought, when those laws are broadly violated by a culture, why should I be surprised that the problems show up in the research? After all, this is my Father's world.

Emboldened, Olivia wrote her term paper on the family. She received a B and the following note from her professor: "I hope I never have to read a paper like this again."

ENDNOTES

1. Patricia Donovan, "A Prescription of Sexually Transmitted Diseases." Issues in Science and Technology (1993). 9:4, p. 40.
2. Robert T. Michael. John H. Gagnon and Edward O. Lauman. Sex in America: A Definitive Survey, (Boston: Little, Brown & Co., 1994) p. 124.
3. Michael et al, p. 125.
4. Jan E. Stets (1993). "The Link Between Past and Present Intimate Relationships," Journal of Family Issues, 114, p. 251.
5. Michael D. Newcomb and P.M. Bentler (1980), "Assessment of Personality and Demographic Aspects of Cohabitation and Marital Success," Journal of Personality Assessment, 44, p. 21.
6. William Axinn and Arland Thorton (1992). "The Relationship Between Cohabitation and Divorce: Selectivity or Casual Influence?" Demography, 29, p. 358.
7. Jan E. Stets (1991), "Cohabiting and Marital Aggression: The Role of Social Isolation," Journal of Marriage and the Family, 53, pp. 669-670.
8. Robert Coombs (1991), "Marital Status and Personal Well-Being: A Literature Review," Family Relations, 40, pp. 97-102.
9. Lee Robins and Darrel Regier, Psychiatric Disorders in America: The Epidemiologic Catchment Area Study (New York: Free Press, 1991), p. 72.
10. Catherine K. Reissman and Naomi Gerstel (1985), "Marital Dissolution and Health: Do Males or Females Have Greater Risk?" Social Science and Medicine, 20, p. 627.
11. U.S. Department of Jusice, Office of Justice Programs. Bureau of Justice Statistics. "Criminal Victimization in the United States, 1992." NCJ-145125. March 1994, p. 31.
12. Sara McLanahan and Gary Sandefur, Growing Up With a Single Parent (Cambridge: Harvard University Press, 1994) p. 1.
13. McLanahan and Sandefur, p. 2.
14. George Rekers, "Research on the Essential Characteristics of the Father's Role for Family Well-Being" Testimony before the Select Committee on Children. Youth and Families, U.S. House of Representatives, 99th Congress, 2nd session, February 25, 1986, pp. 59-60.
15. David Popenoe, "The Controversial Truth," New York Times, December 26, 1992, A-21.
16. Frank F. Furstenberg Jr., "History and Current Status of Divorce in the United States," The Future of Children, 4, no. 1 (Center for the Future of Children, spring 1994), p. 37.
17. David Blankenhorn, Fatherless America: Confronting Our Most Urgent Social Problem (New York: Basic Books, 1995), p. 307.
18. James Egan, M.D., "When Fathers Are Absent." Address given at the National Summit on Fatherhood, sponsored by the National Fatherhood Initiative: Dallas, October 27, 1994.

—Glenn T. Stanton is the director for Family Formation Studies at Focus on the Family in Colorado Springs, Colorado and a research fellow at the Institute of Marriage and Family in Ottawa. He debates and lectures extensively on the issues of gender, sexuality, marriage and parenting at universities and churches around the country. Stanton is the author of five books and a contributor to nine others, including *Why Marriage Matters: Reasons to Believe in Marriage in Postmodern Society, My Crazy, Imperfect Christian Family,* and *Marriage on Trial: The Case Against Same-Sex Marriage and Parenting.*

LESSON 4

COVENANT RELATIONSHIPS

MAIN PRINCIPLE

A covenant is a permanent agreement involving the total being of the persons concerned. When we marry we form a blood covenant with our mate in the eyes of God. Marriage is a covenant relationship that brings with it all the benefits and responsibilities of a blood covenant.

COVENANT RELATIONSHIPS

Complied by ZOE Ministries International

"For this reason a man will leave father and mother and be united to his wife, and they shall become one flesh" Genesis 2:24. This verse includes the phrase "be united to" or, in other translations, "to cleave unto." This means "to cling to, to follow close or to adhere to."[1] It means to stick like glue. It implies a permanent and unbreakable relationship. Marriage is a covenant relationship that requires commitment to one mate for life.

God intended that marriage be entered into not as a contract, but as a covenant. "A contract is an agreement made in suspicion. The parties do not trust each other, and they set "limits" to their own responsibility. A covenant is an agreement made in trust. The parties love each other and put no limits on their own responsibility."[2]

Forming a covenant meant making all you possessed—your skills, strength and all of your material belongings—available to the other party. It also meant the sharing of all your liabilities and debts. Usually a covenant was made for mutual benefit and the assets and liabilities shared were fairly equal.[3]

God has made many covenants with mankind down through the ages. These covenants were not equal. God, the Creator of the universe, had much more to offer. Mankind, with our human nature, came loaded with liabilities. It was God's love and concern for us that caused Him to make covenants with mankind.

The types of covenant we will look at here will be the blood covenant and the marriage covenant. The blood covenant is the strongest, most binding covenant between two people, two nations, or between God and mankind.[4] The tie it created was considered stronger than ties between family members.[5] One just did not break a blood covenant agreement. Breaking a covenant meant sure death and disgrace for one's family.

God instituted the blood covenant. The first blood covenant was with Adam and Eve. An animal was sacrificed to provide a covering for them. Blood was shed and God stated the covenant terms in Genesis 3:14–21. This blood covenant was a type and shadow of the future blood covenant of Jesus (Hebrews 10:29).

The term covenant comes from the Hebrew word berith, which means "to cut."[6] There were many ways to "cut" a blood covenant. They all involved the shedding of blood. Here are some of the ways that the ancients cut a covenant:

a. Cutting somewhere on the body, like the palms, wrists, legs or chests, and clasping them together so that the blood mingled. Sometimes gunpowder or ashes were rubbed into the incisions to leave a scar as evidence of the covenant made.[7]

b. Cutting somewhere on the body, allowing the blood from the two people to flow and be mixed. This mixture would then be drunk, alone or mixed with another liquid.[8]

c. Cutting an animal and using its blood to make the covenant.

All of these methods were used by pagans in the past and also by some cultures today. God employed the cutting of Abraham and his descendants in circumcision as a sign of His covenant with them (Genesis 17:11). God used the spilling of an animal's blood for the atonement of sins for the Israelites.

The importance and significance of blood is stated in Leviticus 17:11–14. (Read from The Amplified Bible.) It says that life is in the blood. The shedding and intermingling of blood, was symbolic of giving one's life and through it two parties became one.[9] Only blood could make atonement for the sins of the people (Romans 3:24–26).

The permanent nature of covenants is referred to in Jeremiah 33: 21–22. Also read Ezekiel 16:8 and Malachi 2:14 to see that marriage is a covenant.

Marriage is a sacred relationship that involves a blood covenant. The sexual union provides the spilling of blood, i.e., when the hymen is broken. (Although, these days it is not uncommon to find a virgin whose hymen has already been torn.) The sexual union consummates the wedding covenant. The couple becomes one flesh. This strongly binding covenant between the man and woman is God's plan for marriage. Read Proverbs 2:17. This underlines the fact that God serves as a witness to this covenant agreement.

A covenant was confirmed by the making of an oath or vow. We continue to observe this practice as we say the wedding vows.

However, some couples now want to write their own vows and they want to drop the "in sickness" clause. They want to share the times of good health, but they don't want to be responsible or committed during times of serious illness or disability of their mate. They drop the "for richer, for poorer" clause because they want the wealth, but not the lack of it. They drop the "until death do us part" clause because they don't want to be committed until death. They don't understand the seriousness and commitment that God's covenant of marriage requires. They don't understand that in this covenant the two partners share both their assets and their liabilities.

Sometimes certain objects were given to signify that a covenant had been made. Remember when Jonathan made a covenant with David, he gave his robe, sword, bow and belt to David in 1 Samuel 18:3–4. Often pieces of jewelry were given. That is why we exchange rings at a wedding ceremony. The rings symbolize the covenant between the man and woman.

After making a blood covenant, a memorial meal was shared. This was an important part of the covenanting process and signified the sharing of life. The covenant partners would feed each other bread and wine saying in effect, "This food and drink are symbolic of my life, my body, and I'm putting it in you."[10] As the bride and groom feed each other wedding cake, they are symbolically saying, "I'm coming into you and you into me. The two of us are becoming one."[11]

Did we all realize we were making a blood covenant when we got married? Maybe not, but God honors our marriage as a blood covenant. Just because we didn't understand doesn't mean it is any less binding of an agreement.[12]

We need to realize that in order for us to be able to keep this covenant with our spouse, we need to have a covenant relationship with God first. It is only after recognizing and accepting the atonement for our sins that God offers through the sacrifice of Jesus, that God can give us what we need to be successful in our marriage relationships. Once we are in covenant with God,

we can then appropriate His strength, wisdom, patience and love for our marriage (Jeremiah 31:31–34).

ENDNOTES

1. James Strong, LL.D., S.T.D., *Strong's Exhaustive Concordance of the Bible* (Nashville, Tennessee: Thomas Nelson Publishers), #1692.
2. Daren Gabriel, "Covenant vs. Contract", www.dariengabriel.com, Friday June 20, 2008.
3. Bonnie Deuschle, "The Blood Covenant" (Harake, Zimbabwe: Rhema Tape Ministries).
4. H. Clay Trumbull, *The Blood Covenant* (Kirkwood, Missouri: Impact Books, Inc., 1975), p. 7.
5. Ibid., p. 17.
6. Strong, #1285.
7. Deuschle.
8. Trumbull, p. 4-8, 17.
9. Richard Booker, *The Miracle of the Scarlet Thread* (Shippensburg, Pennsylvania: Destiny Image Publishers, 1981), p. 29.
10. Ibid., pp. 30-31.
11. Ibid., p. 27.
12. Deuschle.

LESSON 5

LIFETIME LOVE AFFAIR

MAIN PRINCIPLE

In order for us to have a lifetime love affair with our mate, we need all five aspects of love to be evident in our marriage. We must love, respect and care for our mate's body as much as we love, respect and care for our own body. As these principles are practiced in our marriage, we can remain faithful to one another.

LOVE . . . IT NEVER FAILS!

by Marilyn Hickey

God loves you. He loves me. We were born out of God's love. In the natural, some people may not have been born out of a love union, but I John 4:7 says that everyone who is born of God knows God and is born of His love. You are a "love child," birthed of the love of God. You received the fullness of God's love the instant you were born again. Let's look at the love God has for us and the love we can have for others.

The word love comes from the Hebrew word *chashaq,* meaning "to join or fasten together." God's love has holding power: it joins you to Him and fastens the two of you together. *Chashaq* also means "to be attached or to cleave." God's love attaches itself to us and clings to us. Next, chashaq means "to delight in doing." God delights in doing things for you because He loves you!

A derivative of the Hebrew word *chashaq* is *chishshuq,* meaning "conjoined as a wheel-spoke or rod connecting the hub with the rim." God's love is the hub of the wheel, and we are the rim. The actions and steps of love are the spokes. The love of God causes us to be connected to each other, forming the Body of Christ. We have become an extension of His love— the extension of God Who is the center of everything.

In the Greek the most commonly used words for love are:

(1) *Eros,* meaning "an erotic love or physical attraction,"

(2) *Phileo,* meaning "friendship or reciprocal love," and

(3) *Agape,* meaning "love that gives and expects nothing in return."

God the Father has *phileo* love for Jesus: "The Father loves the Son and has given all things into his Hand; . . ." (John 3:35). Then in John 16:27, Jesus says that God loves believers with *phileo* love: "For the Father Himself loveth you, because you have loved me, and have believed that I came out from God." This is reciprocal love—love that hopes for a return.

Agape love, on the other hand, is the love from which we were reborn. This unselfish love comes from heaven itself, because God gives and expects nothing back: "For God so loved the world, that He gave His only begotten Son, . . ." (John 3:16). God loves sinners – although they don't love Him in return. He loved you before you were born again. *Agape* love is a fruit of the Spirit: it is patient, kind, rejoices in the truth, believes all things, hopes all things, and endures all things. *Agape* love never fails.

Ephesians 5:2 says we are to walk in the agape type of love. But how can we do that? By staying connected to the hub, God's love, we make the wheels of our life go around – instead of collapsing! Here are the spokes of love that connect us to the Father:

SPOKE #1

We must be committed to God's Word and abide in love. Unless we are committed to the Word and keep His commandments, we will never be able to walk in love. What are God's commandments? His Word! Keeping His Word causes you to abide in love (John 15:10). If we will keep His Word, His love will be matured in us. So, we have to make a quality decision to obey the Word above all else in order to walk in God's love.

SPOKE #2

We must provoke one another to love (Hebrews 10:24). To provoke comes from the Greek word paroxusmos, meaning "to incite or urge." What happens as we speak the truth in love to each other? A spiritual cement comes out of us that glues us together in the Body (Ephesians 4:15, 16). We need to learn to provoke people to love so we can be "fitted and held together by that which every joint supplies."

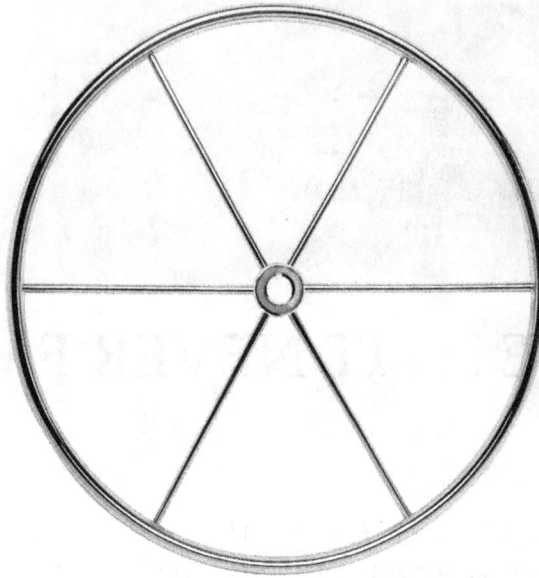

5:6 says "For in Jesus Christ neither circumcision availeth any thing, nor uncircumcision; but faith which worketh by love." Our faith comes through hearing the Word of God. As we fill our hearts with God's Word and begin to speak it, our minds and emotions line up with the Word. But if we don't have love, our faith will fail us—we are as a noisy gong or a clanging cymbal (I Corinthians 13:1). Love never fails! Faith, hope, and love all abide in us through God's Word - but the greatest of these is love!

SPOKE #3

Act in love – love is shown by the actions it prompts. How do we activate love? How can we have overcoming love? According to Deuteronomy 30:14-16, we need to love God and walk in His ways – we need to keep His Word in our mouths: "But the word is very nigh unto thee, in thy mouth, and in thy heart, that thou art mayest do it. See, I have set before thee this day life and good, and death and evil; In that I command thee this day to love the LORD thy God, to walk in his ways, and to keep his commandments and his statutes and his judgments, that thou mayest live and multiply: and the LORD thy God shall bless thee in the land whither thou goest to possess it."

Jesus walked in love in every situation—even when others were angry at Him. In Luke 4:28-30, the people were "filled with wrath" at Jesus and carried Him off to a hill so they could throw Him over a cliff! But Jesus didn't fight back; He released the power of love and passed through their midst.

In essence Jesus turned the other cheek and released the power of God to protect Him from His enemies. When you don't return anger to people who are angry with you, you release the power of God's love. There is great power in love.

SPOKE #4

Stay in love to make your faith work. Galatians

SPOKE #5

Know God loves you. There is a confidence in our spirits when we are loving and know that God loves us. When we know we have repented of our sins and Jesus lives in our hearts, we are confident that He loves us (I John 3:18-21). When we're confident, we're not condemned, we know we receive of Him. Receive God's love for you today!

SPOKE #6

Love others with God's love, for love prevents sin. I Peter says, "Above all, keep fervent in your love for one another, because love covers a multitude of sins." To cover means "to prevent." God's love will prevent sin among us, and our love for God will keep us from sinning.

HOLY RELATIONSHIPS OF LOVE

Although we are loved totally and completely by the Trinity, the Father, Son, and Holy Spirit each love us differently. Let's look at their specific loves in our lives:

John 14:21-23 shows the love of the Father. Jesus said that if we keep the commandments and love Him, the Father will love us. As we keep His Word, Jesus and the Father will abide in us. The Father loves us!

Hebrews 12 states that God chastens us for our

good because He loves us. In this verse to chasten means "to train." It doesn't mean that God is going to beat us to a pulp. God manifested a father's love in begetting us. What does the father of a household usually do? He disciplines and trains his children. God chastens us with His Word.

Let's look at Jesus' love for us. Jesus laid down everything He had and gave His life for us (I John 3:16).

There is "love" fellowship with Jesus. He knows us as humans and as brothers; He knows all about us but still loves us:

"Wherefore in all things it behoved him to be made like unto his brethren, that he might be a merciful and faithful high priest in things pertaining to God, to make reconciliation for the sins of the people. For in that he himself hath suffered being tempted, he is able to succour them that are tempted" (Hebrews 2:17, 18).

Our relationship to the Holy Spirit's love can be compared to a mother-child relationship. The mother of a family gives birth and then trains and teaches the children. The Spirit calls the sinner, woos, and draws him or her into the new birth. Then the Holy Spirit leads us and trains us in God's truth.

A mother sets her children apart; she separates them from other children who may influence them negatively The Spirit sanctifies you: "And when he (the Holy Spirit) is come, he will reprove the world of sin, and of righteousness, and of judgment" (John 16:8).

Finally, a mother comforts her children when they are hurt. The Holy Spirit is called the "Comforter": "And I will pray the Father, and he shall give you another comforter, that he may abide with you for ever" (John 14:16).

You may ask, "Marilyn, why do we have all of these kinds of love?" Because we need them! The three kinds of love from God are each unique and fulfill a specific role in our lives—the discipline of a father, the training and comfort of a mother, and the fellowship of a brother.

As we let God's love fill us up, it can flow out of us to help the rest of the Body. God's love is shed abroad in our hearts as we walk in His ways—the spokes—of love. As we draw from His love, we make the world go around. People will be drawn to God by the love you show them. Your human love may fail, but God's love emanating from you will always succeed!

—Marilyn Hickey is an American minister and Christian television personality who teaches Bible studies both nationally and internationally. She and her husband Wallace founded the Orchard Road Christian Center, a large church in Denver, Colorado.

Reprinted by permission: Marilyn Hickey Ministries

FIVE GREATEST NEEDS IN MARRIAGE

1. List the five greatest needs you have in marriage.

    a.

    b.

    c.

    d.

    e.

2. List what you think your spouse's five greatest needs in marriage are.

    a.

    b.

    c.

    d.

    e.

FIVE GREATEST NEEDS IN MARRIAGE

1. List the five greatest needs you have in marriage.

    a.

    b.

    c.

    d.

    e.

2. List what you think your spouse's five greatest needs in marriage are.

    a.

    b.

    c.

    d.

    e.

LESSON 6

PRESCRIPTION FOR A SUPERB MARRIAGE

MAIN PRINCIPLE

God intends that a husband and wife should enjoy sexual union within the guidelines He has given. As we choose to act and think lovingly towards our mate, trust and understanding deepens, enhancing our love relationship.

ROMANCING YOUR MARRIAGE

by H. Norman Wright

As each person gives and receives positive loving acts, the bond of love will grow stronger.

Have you ever experienced a love recession in your marriage? Some of you know what I'm talking about, but others may be a bit threatened by what I'm going to say. There are times when marital love is intense, strong and vibrant. But there are also times when you begin to question your love for your spouse or your spouse's love for you.

For some reason love recedes from a previously higher and more fulfilling level. Sometimes this occurs at predictable stages in marriage, such as honeymoon, childbearing, empty nest and so on. It can happen after two years of marriage, or 20 years, or 40 years. Yes, just like a financial recession, a love recession can even happen to Christians who think their marriage will only climb upward.

When people feel that their love (or their partner's love) is weakening, they experience a multitude of feelings. A love recession can be frightening, frustrating and even depressing. Anxiety rises and you look for an answer. It can be threatening for a couple to face up to a sense of diminishing love, but it can also become a time of positive growth.

It is like a financial crisis in which the way you respond can have a large bearing on your survival. Unlike the victim of a financial recession, however, you are never bankrupt of currency in a love recession. You never run out of love. You just need to look for it in some new places so you can grow and develop new love in your relationship.

When a love recession occurs, you may feel alone or isolated and think that something is wrong with you. You begin questioning whether you ever loved your partner in the first place and wondering if the diminished love can ever become strong again.

No, you are not the only person who has ever experienced this phenomenon. Don't panic. And don't ignore what is happening. One of the unhealthiest ways to respond is to ignore or deny what is occurring. These experiences and feelings happen to many couples. It is important to remember that, with honest acceptance of the situation and some positive action, your love can and will increase. So what can you do when a love recession hits?

You can allow a love recession to devastate you, or you can respond to it as a time of growth and change. If and when a love recession hits, accept what you are experiencing and feeling as something that is quite normal. Don't deny your feelings. Instead, write them down—both positive and negative. Set up a convenient appointment to communicate your feelings. Then lovingly share the entire range of your thoughts and feelings with your partner, not as an ultimatum for them to change, but as a point of information signaling your interest in making your marriage stronger.

Evaluate your thought life toward yourself and your partner over recent months. Evaluate your behavior and your partner's behavior over that time and be sure you give yourselves credit for the positives. We all have a tendency to focus on defects, failures and negatives rather than on the positives, even though the positives often outweigh the negatives.

Consciously try some new loving behaviors toward your partner. Make a special effort to act out your love even if the feelings of love are not as strong as they once were.

February 1988, Charisma

Consider the various ways of expressing your love to your partner which are suggested in this article.

One very practical way is through touching. I'm not talking here about erotic sexual caressing and fondling which leads into the bedroom. Rather I am referring to daily acts of physical contact which are ends of romance, love and communication in themselves.

Don't get me wrong—I'm in favor of sexual touching in marriage. But over the years I have heard hundreds of women tell why they do not respond to their husbands' touching. It's not because they don't enjoy sex. But as one woman puts it, whose comments reflect the feelings of many other women, "When he caresses me, hugs me or strokes my hand, I know what he has in mind. I wish he could give me affection without an ulterior motive. I enjoy sex, but he doesn't realize that the casual touches during the day can lead to greater sex in the bedroom!" Very well stated.

Hugging is an important element of touching. And hugging is a vital expression of love. Do you hug your spouse and others? Do you receive hugs? One of my favorite quotes is, "Every marriage needs to be picked up and hugged and given personal attention." Hugging is a preventative and cure for love recession.

Another way to keep love alive and fight recession is to bless your spouse. What? Yes, bless your spouse—and I don't mean, "Bless that so and so, grrr...." I mean speaking a blessing in a positive way. The word "blessing" in the New Testament is based on two Greek words which mean "well" and "word." Blessing your spouse literally means to speak well of that person.

You can bless your partner by what you say to him/her and how you say it. You should speak lovingly and encouragingly in order to make your mate's life fuller, not out of a sense of duty. You can build up your spouse by becoming his/her greatest fan. You are in the front row of the grandstand for your partner's every endeavor, cheering, "Go for it! You can do it! I believe in you!"

Your verbal response to your partner's words is important. Saying thank you, expressing appreciation and offering requested information or opinions with kindness will bless your mate. And the ultimate way of verbally blessing your partner is to lift that person to the Lord in prayer and intervene on his/her behalf.

As you edify your spouse in this way you will increase his/her sense of self-worth. The result will be an increase in your spouse's capacity to give of himself/herself to you in love.

I like the ways Ed Wheat suggests for building up partners:

1. Make a decision to never again be critical of your partner in thought, word and deed. This should be a decision backed up by action until it becomes a habit that you would not change even if you could.

2. Spend time studying your spouse so you develop a sensitivity to the areas in which the person feels a lack. Discover creative ways to build your spouse up in those weak areas.

3. Spend time thinking daily of positive qualities and behavior patterns you admire and appreciate in your spouse. Make a list and thank God for these.

4. Consistently verbalize praise and appreciation, and do this in a specific and generous manner.

5. Recognize what your spouse does, but also who your spouse is. Let him or her know that you respect them for what they accomplish.

6. Husbands, publicly and privately show your wife how special she is to you. Keep your attention focused on your wife and not on other women.

7. Wives, show your husband how important he is in your life. Ask his opinion and value his judgments.

8. Respond to each other physically and facially. Our faces are the most expressive parts of us. Smile with your total face. Your spouse needs to receive more of your smiles than others.

9. Be courteous to each other in private and in public. Each of you should be a VIP in your home.

I have talked with many couples who feel that they have tried to demonstrate love and meet the needs of their spouses but keep missing the mark. To eliminate misunderstanding and mind reading, it is far better to share with one another your needs, wants and desires in a specific, yet non-demanding manner. When you seek to learn your partner's wishes in order to meet them as best you can, you are implementing the model of servanthood as portrayed in the Scripture.

One of the most effective ways of meeting each other's love needs and wants is to launch into the "Cherishing Days" exercise. Sound interesting? It can be very interesting, and it is easy to implement.

February 1988, Charisma

Each partner makes a list of small cherishing behaviors which he or she would enjoy receiving from the other. These requested behaviors should have four characteristics:

1. They must be specific and positive. For example, Janice would like Jim to sit next to her on the couch as they watch the news after dinner. Janice has made a positive request for a desired behavior instead of complaining, "You ignore me and are preoccupied with the TV."
2. The small cherishing behaviors must not be concerned with past conflicts or old demands.
3. The positive behaviors must be such that they can be accomplished on an everyday basis.
4. The behaviors must be achievable—they do not require excessive time or expense.

Take several days to compile your lists. Think back to the most satisfying times of your courtship and marriage to discover ideas for your list. Some of the behaviors you think of may seem trivial or somewhat embarrassing to you. It's perfectly all right. Include them on your list as long as they reflect valid personal wants or needs.

Once your list of 15-20 cherishing behaviors is completed, exchange lists with your partner and discuss the cherishing behaviors you are requesting from each other. Be sure to tell your spouse how you would like each behavior performed for you. For example, if you request a back rub at bedtime, specify light skin rub or deep muscle massage, with lotion or without, etc. As you discuss your written behaviors, feel free to add others to the list as you think of them.

After your discussion, declare the next seven days to be "Cherishing Days." Make a commitment to put your partner's list into practice. Try to accomplish as many of the cherishing behaviors on the list as possible each day. Focus your attention and energies on what you do for your spouse, not what he/she does for you. At the end of seven days, you may evaluate whether you will continue the exercise for another week.

Why does this work so well to encourage love and romance? Because the list of positive behaviors which you exchange consists of requested, discussed and agreed upon acts of love. The guesswork of "What shall I do for him/her? Will he/she like it?" is eliminated. Also, the commitment is short term—you are only responsible for seven days. And the behaviors are purposely simple and easily achievable. The margin of failure is greatly reduced.

Another important factor in the success of this exercise is the commitment of each individual to the "I must change first" principle. You are not keeping score of your spouse's efforts. You are too busy concentrating on accomplishing his/her list. And with each behavior comes a positive response, which encourages the giver to continue. As each person gives and receives positive loving acts, the bond of love will grow stronger.

Most couples decide to continue the exercise after completing the seven-day commitment. They find that the positives of fulfilling each other's wants and needs eliminate the negatives of love-recessive behavior patterns.

Dating is vital in the process of courtship and perhaps even more important in marriage as an antidote to love recession.

Quite often as I work with couples in counseling I encourage them to date one another. "Where do we go on a date?" they ask. "How do I know what he or she would like to do on a date?" The first step in answering these questions is to conduct a date interview. When your spouse is in a relaxed mood or when the two of you are out to dinner, say, "I need 10 minutes of your time to conduct an interview with you. I can't tell you what it is for at this time, but you will eventually know more about it." Then ask your spouse the following questions:

1. When you used to date in high school or college, what were your favorite types of dates? Why?
2. During those years, did you dream about an outstanding date that you always wanted to have but never did? (I don't mean with a certain movie star!)
3. What are your favorite colors?
4. What is your favorite type of music?
5. What are your favorite travel spots to visit?
6. What are your favorite foods?
7. What type of restaurant do you like best?
8. What are your three favorite desserts?
9. What are your favorite flowers?
10. What is your favorite cologne/perfume?
11. What are your favorite types of books?
12. What shows or plays do you enjoy the most and why?
13. What three types of activities would you like to try, given a chance to do so?

February 1988, Charisma

The results of the interview should give you ample ideas for numerous dates which incorporate many of your partner's "favorites."

Did you know that former president Harry Truman was a dyed-in-the-wool romantic? He pursued his wife, Bess, for many years before she agreed to marry him. He first asked her in 1911, and they were finally married in 1919. But once he married her, Mr. Truman continued to romance his wife. When he was away from her, he wrote love letters. And when Bess Truman died in the early 1980s, more than 1,200 letters from her husband were discovered in her home. Harry never stopped courting Bess.

Did you write any love letters to each other when you were courting? If so, did you save any? Find them and enjoy an evening together reading old love letters to each other. You can still write love letters too. Spend some time creating your letter and then inscribe it on some kind of special paper. Perhaps you could send it to your spouse's work place, but be sure to mark it "Personal." Or you could hand deliver it to your spouse in a romantic setting.

Here is a portion of a touching love letter written by Ingrid Trobisch to her husband, Walter, who published the excerpt in his book, All a Man Can Be:

"I want to tell you why I love you. When I picture you in my mind, I can see you stretching out your hand to me. I trust your hand for it is the hand of a safe and secure man. It is true, you walk a little ahead of me, but when you realize I'm getting out of breath and can't quite keep up, you stand still. You turn around and give me your hand to help me over hard places. Then I come very near to you and you talk to me and comfort me. You don't make fun of my thoughts, neither are you threatened by them if they challenge you to try a new path.

When I am weak and need protection, I know that you are stronger than I, and so I take hold of your hand because I know that you will never use your strength to make me feel inferior.

But you need me, too, and you are not ashamed to show it. Even though you are strong and manly, you can also be helpless as a child. Your strong hand can then become an open, empty hand. And I know no greater happiness than to fill it."

We can do no better than imitate the Trobisch's mutual affection. With resources such as warmth, touch, personal care, encouragement and enjoyment, why should we put up with love recessions? And we can bank on the Holy Spirit to help us learn to love one another.

—H. Norman Wright is a licensed Marriage, Family and Child Therapist and was in private practice for over thirty years. Wright has taught in the Graduate Department of Biola University. He is the author of over seventy books.

Reprinted by permission Charisma Magazine and Strang Communications Company.

February 1988, Charisma

LESSON 7

TRUE ROMANCE

MAIN PRINCIPLE

There can be true romance in our marriage no matter how long or short a time we have been married. We can learn how to restore or improve the romance in our marriage.

MEN: DATE YOUR WIVES

by Eric Geiger

While there is not a biblical mandate to have a date night every week with your spouse, there is the command to love your wife as Christ loved you (Eph. 5:25). And how did He love us? He pursued us when our hearts were cold to Him. He continually wooed us to Himself. He offered Himself fully for us to establish an everlasting relationship, one that will endure for all time.

Men often stop pursuing and dating their wives with the same passion with which they initially pursued them. And this is a poor reflection of the greater marriage we have with Christ.

When God confronted the church at Ephesus, He rebuked them for losing their first love (Rev. 2:4) and challenged them to do the things they did at first (2:5). They had lost their intimate walk with the Lord, and He was calling them to repentance. There is a connection between losing your first love and stopping the things you did at first (time with the Lord, sensitivity to His Spirit, daily repentance, etc.). When applied to a marriage, the same is true. There is a connection between drifting from love expressed to our spouse and the stopping of things we did at first.

In other words, men, date your wife.

Early in our marriage, as a newlywed couple in college, Kaye and I committed to have a date night every week and a vacation together every year. I made 12K a year as a student pastor, and she worked part-time at a bank, so funding was the main challenge for our date nights. Thus, our two favorite places to eat were the Pizza Inn buffet and the Shoney's breakfast bar (our metabolism was a lot higher back then).

We didn't have a comfortable couch, so when it was cold outside, we would rent a movie and snuggle on a twin mattress we placed in front of our TV. When it was warm, we often spread out in a hammock we had hanging in our yard and talked. With kids, the challenges change, but our commitment to a date night is the same. Here are five tips we have learned.

1. **Schedule it.** If we don't schedule the date each week, it won't happen. So we plan several days out and block off the time. Sometimes she initiates and reminds me in a loving and subtle way, without making me feel like a loser husband for forgetting. Other times I am the one to say, "Hey, what night do you want to go out this week?"

2. **Start again.** Some weeks we miss. Instead of assuming our marriage is falling apart or letting that miss become a habit, we simply pick back up the next week.

3. **Kid swap.** We have never enjoyed the luxury of living in the same city as our parents, so we know the babysitting cost can be a challenge. When we lived in Miami, we had a weekly kid swap with another couple. One week they would go out and my wife would go to their house so their kids could go to bed on time in their own beds. The next week it would be our turn to go out. On the weeks when it was the other couple's turn, we would have an "in-house date" with takeout and a movie.

4. **Explore.** It is easy to fall into the same routine with the same restaurant each week. For us, we have enjoyed exploring new parts of the city where we live,

February 14, 2013, Charisma

eating at local places, and checking out areas we have not yet conquered.

5. **Romance.** You don't have to wait until you are home to kiss and hold your wife. Find some places where you can talk, embrace, and enjoy each other. In Miami, we would pull the car up next to the water on Key Biscayne, snuggle while listening to jazz at Van Dykes, etc. I am not giving away my Nashville spots. Men, dating your wife is spiritual. Do the things you did at first. And enjoy it!

—Eric Geiger serves as the Vice President of the Church Resource Division at LifeWay Christian Resources. He is also a teaching pastor and a frequent speaker and consultant on church mission and strategy. Eric authored or co-authored several books including the best-selling church leadership book, Simple Church.

Reprinted by permission Charisma Magazine and Strang Communications Company.

February 14, 2013, Charisma

SPENDING TIME

by Skip Heitzig

A man was having problems in his relationship with his wife, so he went to a marriage counselor. The counselor said, "You need to learn how to listen to what your wife says. Understand what she's communicating." A month later, he came back and said, "OK, I've done it. I've learned to listen to every word my wife says." The counselor said, "That's a good start. Now go home and listen to what she doesn't say. Listen to her heart."

In Proverbs 5:18 Solomon says, very beautifully and poetically, "Let your fountain be blessed, and rejoice with the wife of your youth." The Hebrew word translated "rejoice" means to brighten up, to cheer up, to be glad, or to be joyful. "Enjoy each other" is the idea, the same thing he expresses in Ecclesiastes when he says, "Live joyfully with the wife whom you love."

Marriage is to be enjoyable, and you are to live joyfully with your spouse. How many people do you know who do that? I know people who live routinely, enduringly, grimacing-ly, with their spouse. But how many live and enjoy each other for a lifetime?

The most obvious thing is to enjoy each other's company. That sounds elementary, and for a couple when they first meet and start dating, it's not an issue. Wild horses can't drag them apart; they want to be together all the time. But as time goes on, and after the vows are said, sometimes that thrill of discovery is gone. They find their mate has idiosyncrasies and annoying habits: "I didn't know you snored!" Silly little things like that.

But the most successful marriages I've ever seen are those who continue to bond with each other by spending time together, enjoying each other's company. Although the immediate context of the passage in Proverbs 5 is sexual bliss within a marriage, understand (and women do understand this!) that it begins a lot earlier than 10 p.m. Someone said, "If you want to have an energized sex life in marriage, try a little tenderness the other 23 and a half hours of the day."

It's all about time spent with each other. Intimacy begins with harmony between a couple as they spend time together. You were really in touch when you first dated and when you were first married. Don't lose touch with each other. Continue to communicate with each other—and that will get harder to do as life gets busier and busier, so you must be committed to it.

It's a challenge. According to research, the average female uses 25,000 words a day, and the average male only about 10,000. If he has used up 9,500 at work, he may feel like he wants to shut down in the evening. So the time with each other can be strained. But I'm speaking about more than words; things like reading each other's body language and listening to each other's heart.

One wife expressed it this way to her husband. "Please come, take my hand. Let's walk. Give me you— eyes that say hi, glances that say I care, hand-holds that let me know you were only teasing, hugs saying 'Thank you for being you,' kisses that gently want me, love that says I'll be here tomorrow and every day hereafter."

That's the kind of sharing that builds emotional intimacy for the long haul!

—Skip Heitzig is senior pastor of Calvary Albuquerque, located in Albuquerque, New Mexico. Heitzig's worldwide multimedia ministry includes a half-hour radio program called "The Connection" and various video documentaries. He has authored several books and writes for The Connection Devotional found at OnePlace.com.

LESSON 8

LET'S COMMUNICATE

MAIN PRINCIPLE

Scripture provides a warning against the evil of an uncontrolled and uncharitable tongue. Our words can either tear down our mate or bless them and build them up. We need to communicate storge *and* phileo *love in our marriage.*

A MATTER OF LIFE AND DEATH

"Death and life are in the power of the tongue, and they who indulge in it shall eat the fruit of it [for life or death]" Proverbs 18:21 (AMP).

If things continually don't seem to go right for you, maybe you need a tongue check. Your tongue can bring you total disaster in any area of your life. What are you saying concerning the following areas? Are you speaking life or death? Mark beside each item an "L" for "life" or "D" for "death."

You, in general—

Your walk with the Lord—

Your mate—

Your children—

Your parents—

Your relatives—

Your friends—

Your employer—

Your employees—

Your home—

Your school—

God's plan and purpose for your life—

The government—

Your nation—

The news media—

Your health—

Your finances—

Your job—

Your future—

Your success—

The weather—

Your church—

Your leaders—

If we have many areas of life in which we marked "D," we are probably communicating negatively to our spouse as well.

A MATTER OF LIFE AND DEATH

"Death and life are in the power of the tongue, and they who indulge in it shall eat the fruit of it [for life or death]" Proverbs 18:21 (AMP).

If things continually don't seem to go right for you, maybe you need a tongue check. Your tongue can bring you total disaster in any area of your life. What are you saying concerning the following areas? Are you speaking life or death? Mark beside each item an "L" for "life" or "D" for "death."

You, in general—   The government—

Your walk with the Lord—   Your nation—

Your mate—   The news media—

Your children—   Your health—

Your parents—   Your finances—

Your relatives—   Your job—

Your friends—   Your future—

Your employer—   Your success—

Your employees—   The weather—

Your home—   Your church—

Your school—   Your leaders—

God's plan and purpose for your life—

If we have many areas of life in which we marked "D," we are probably communicating negatively to our spouse as well.

LEARN FROM EACH OTHER

by Richard D. Dobbins

"Can we talk?" Unfortunately, for many of the parsonage couples seeking my help with marriage problems, their answer is "No, we can't talk."

However, if you and your spouse have problems communicating with each other, it's not likely your marriage is to blame. Marriage doesn't cause poor communication—it reveals it.

Literate societies, such as ours, stress the importance of reading and writing in their formal education programs. However, people are given little training in speaking and listening – essential skills in revealing intimate feelings so vital to marriage.

No wonder 80 percent of couples in the ministry who seek my help in resolving their marital problems put poor communication at the top of their list!

The most important skill in building a healthy marriage is the art of compassionate listening. Once we learn to listen with compassion, we begin to hear things from the other person's point of view. What a difference this makes! Giant strides in understanding are bound to follow.

Why is it so difficult for husbands and wives to listen to each other with understanding? They are frustrated by the gender barrier— the difficulty a husband and wife experience in trying to imagine how the world is perceived by the opposite sex.

Men give very little thought to what it might have been like to grow up as a female—and very few women have wondered what little boys experience as they grow up to be men. If you aren't tuned in to the other's point of view, how can you hope to understand each other? No man knows what it is like to be a woman—and no woman knows what it is like to be a man.

A father should teach his son what he has learned about a woman's world from the boy's mother. And a mother should teach her daughter what she has learned bout the man's world from the girl's father. However, it's the rare family where that kind of open communication exists between parents and children.

Therefore, most couples must be humble enough to learn from each other. If I am ever to know what a woman's world is like, I must be willing to learn from my wife. And if she is to discover a man's world, she must be willing to learn from me. When a couple learns these invaluable perspectives from each other, they are well on their way into a new dimension of intimacy.

A second essential skill in the art of listening is the ability to listen for understanding. What is meant is not always apparent from what is said.

The insecure hearer often jumps to inaccurate conclusions by confusing what is said for what is meant. It is very hard to relax around this kind of person and speak freely. Every word must be weighed very carefully.

On the other hand, people who listen with compassion and for understanding put us at ease. We don't have to watch every word we say. Why not learn to listen to your partner this way?

Now let's focus on some speaking skills. First, look at the skill of mental rehearsal.

"My dear brothers, take note of this: Everyone should be quick to listen, slow to speak and slow to become angry" (James 1:19, NIV). Good marital advice!

James is encouraging us to hear carefully and to choose our words wisely. How do you do that? You mentally determine what you want to say. Then you put yourself in the place of the hearer and imagine his or her reaction.

By mentally alternating between the roles of speaker and hearer, you can silently practice what you want to say, editing it in your mind as many times as is necessary. This is the kind of patient process which builds healthy marital communication.

In other words, don't "shoot from the lip!" Don't think with your mouth! Careless words, impulsively spoken, can cost you hours of painful attempts to explain what you meant—sometimes into the middle of the night. Eventually, such carelessness can even destroy your marriage.

Secondly, learn to express yourself in ways that are not so dogmatic. This will allow your spouse to differ from you without feeling wrong, dumb or rejected.

If you will work on these communication skills, which are simply practical Christian ways of expressing yourself, you and your spouse will begin to feel more at ease with each other and your relationship will thrive.

—Dr. Richard D. Dobbins, ordained by the Assemblies of God, founded and served as CEO of EMERGE Ministries in Akron, OH. Dobbins has authored over 50 books, articles and other media in the United States as well as several foreign countries. He has lectured at universities and led hundreds of seminars and has also served on numerous non-profit boards.

LESSON 9

LET'S COMMUNICATE (CONTINUED)

MAIN PRINCIPLE

Scripture provides a warning against the evil of an uncontrolled and uncharitable tongue. Our words can either tear down our mate or bless them and build them up. We need to communicate agape *love in our marriage.*

TAMING THE TONGUE

1. Results of an Out-Of-Control Tongue

a. **Proverbs 12:18–19** and **Galatians 5:15**—Hurting people around you

b. **Proverbs 15:4**—Crushing someone's spirit

c. **Proverbs 25:23 (AMP)**—Causing others to be angry

d. **Proverbs 17:20**—Falling into trouble

e. **Proverbs 10:19**—Producing sin in your life

f. **Matthew 15:18**—Being unclean in God's eyes

g. **Jeremiah 9:3–9** and **Matthew 12:36–37**—Incurring God's judgment

2. How to Tame the Tongue

a. **Deuteronomy 30:19–20a**—Choose life

b. **Isaiah 30:15**—Repent

c. **Luke 6:45** and **Ezekiel 18:30–32**—Get a new heart. The tongue cannot be tamed until the heart is changed.

Psalm 119:11	
Proverbs 4:20–24	Read, meditate on and
Hebrews 4:12–13	memorize God's Word.
Psalm 19:14	
Psalm 86:11	Ask God in prayer for a new heart and
Psalm 141:3	control of your speech.
1 Thessalonians 5:16–18	Choose to express gratitude and
Philippians 4:4–7	rejoice in the Lord.

d. **Proverbs 15:4**—Ask, "Will what I want to say build up or tear down my spouse?" Be watchful.

e. **Exodus 14:14 "The Lord will fight for you; you need only to be still."** Sacrifice. If what you were going to say is destructive, give it up.

3. Results of a Spirit-Controlled Tongue

a. **Proverbs 21:23**—Protection from calamity

b. **Psalm 126:1–3**—A grateful and joyful life

c. **Psalm 40:9–10**—Praise for God, which can direct other people toward Him

d. **Proverbs 12:25**—The ability to cheer up your spouse

e. **Psalm 49:3**—Wisdom that helps your family

f. **Proverbs 12:18**—Healing for your mate through wise words

g. **1 Corinthians 14:3**—Strength, encouragement and comfort for your spouse through a prophetic word

h. **Isaiah 50:4**—Help for your spouse when he/she is weary

i. **Numbers 6:22–27**—Blessings from God for your spouse

j. **Psalm 34:12–13**—Days filled with life and goodness

LET'S COMMUNICATE
FIRST COUPLE

The goal of this leson is to become better friends and companions, and to learn to communicate our needs with each other.

We are going to role-play several family situations. Your job is to read and set the scene from the argument below. Afterwards, discuss with the class the common blunders found in this conversation and a more helpful way to communicate this situation.

HUSBAND:
"DON'T DO THAT! DON'T YOU KNOW HOW TO DO ANYTHING RIGHT? CAN'T YOU GET JUST ONE THING STRAIGHT? DO I HAVE TO TELL YOU EVERYTHING—ALL THE TIME?"

WIFE:
"AND YOU THINK YOU DO THINGS RIGHT? WHAT ABOUT THE TIME YOU SAVED US $200 BY FIXING THE CAR YOURSELF AND FORGOT TO PUT THE FLUID BACK IN THE TRANSMISSION? THAT COST US OVER $1200 TO REPAIR. THAT WAS REAL SMART!".

LET'S COMMUNICATE
SECOND COUPLE

The goal of this lesson is to become better friends and companions, and to learn to communicate our needs with each other.

We are going to role-play several family situations. Your job is to read and set the scene from the argument below. Afterwards discuss with the class the common blunders found in this conversation and a more helpful way to communicate in this situation.

WIFE:
"I JUST FEEL OVERWHELMED. WHEN I GET UP, I FEEL LIKE I'M FACED WITH A HUNDRED THINGS TO DO. AND I FEEL LIKE **I** HAVE TO DO THEM ALL!"

HUSBAND:
"HERE WE GO AGAIN! I HELP OUT AROUND HERE! HOW MUCH MORE AM I SUPPOSED TO DO? I HELP OUT ALL THE TIME. GET OFF MY CASE. I'M NOT EVEN OUT OF BED YET AND WE ARE ALREADY IN A FIGHT!"

LET'S COMMUNICATE
THIRD COUPLE

The goal of this lesson is to become better friends and companions, and to learn to communicate our needs with each other.

We are going to role-play several family situations. Your job is to read and set the scene from the argument below. Afterwards discuss with the class the common blunders found in this conversation and a more helpful way to communicate in this situation.

WIFE:
"YOU SOUND JUST LIKE MY FATHER! YOU KNOW THAT MAKES ME MAD, AND YOU JUST KEEP ON AND ON!! HE USED TO DO THAT VERY SAME THING TO ME, AND I HATE IT!"

HUSBAND:
"TOUGH! AM NOT YOUR FATHER! AND, IF I SOUND LIKE HIM, THATS TOO BAD. BUT THATS HOW I FEEL ABOUT IT, AND I´M NOT GOING TO CHANGE!"

LET'S COMMUNICATE
FOURTH COUPLE

The goal of this lesson is to become better friends and companions, and to learn to communicate our needs with each other.

We are going to role-play several family situations. Your job is to read and set the scene from the argument below. Afterwards discuss with the class the common blunders found in this conversation and a more helpful way to communicate in this situation.

HUSBAND:
"YOU ARE <u>ALWAYS</u> TALKING ON THE PHONE. OTHERS <u>ALWAYS</u> SEEM SO MUCH MORE IMPORTANT TO YOU THAN ME! THIS ALSO INCLUDES OUR KIDS—YOU <u>ALWAYS</u> PUT THEM FIRST!"

WIFE:
"YOU <u>ALWAYS</u> SAY '<u>ALWAYS</u>' WHENEVER I DO THINGS THAT DON'T PLEASE YOU. YOU ARE <u>ALWAYS</u> ACCUSING ME OF THINGS I DON'T DO. WHY DON'T YOU EXAMINE YOURSELF FIRST INSTEAD OF ALWAYS ACCUSING ME?!"

HOW TO DONATE TO ZOE MINISTRIES

Help us deliver the message of Life throughout the World!

In addition to providing support for ZOE missions, curriculum development/translation and course scholarships, many of our translated materials will be donated to believers without resources to purchase them.

Would you prayerfully consider supporting this ministry?

YOU ARE ABLE TO MAKE A DONATION IN ANY OF THE FOLLOWING WAYS:

Online with PayPal Account or Credit Card via PayPal

This gives you a safe and easy way to make designated contributions.

Visit our website to make a secure online donation.
www.zoeministries.org

By Automatic Bill Pay

Recurring donations to ZOE or to a designated ZOE missionary may be set up with your bank.

By Check

Please make checks payable to 'ZOE Ministries International'
Please don't write a missionary's name on the check. Instead include a separate note.
Our Address is – PO Box 2207, Arvada CO 80001-2207, USA

.

May God bless you richly for your support of this ministry!

"Now this is eternal life [zoe]: that they may know you, the only true God, and Jesus Christ, whom you have sent." - John 17:3

LESSON 10

FREEDOM THROUGH FORGIVENESS

MAIN PRINCIPLE

Forgiveness heals the marital relationship and
frees us to establish a loving, healthy marriage.

HEALING HURTING MARRIAGES

by Dr. Stephen and Judy King

Good marriages don't just happen; they are the result of time, energy and commitment to God and to each other!

The Scripture states, "Therefore shall a man leave his father and mother and shall cleave unto his wife; and they shall be one flesh" (Gen. 2:24). Becoming one is a lifetime process. When sin entered the world, we became selfish and self-centered. Adam pointed a finger at Eve; and she, in turn, pointed her finger at the serpent. Each one projected the blame on someone else for the purpose of self-preservation. The concept of self-preservation clearly hinders the "cleaving" of one marriage partner to the other and becoming one in the spirit.

A successful marriage consists of companionship, romance, serving and sexual fulfillment. These four areas are important components of our human make-up, and they determine whether a relationship grows stronger or dies.

WHERE IS THE ROMANCE?

Emotions, excitement, attraction and affection are all part of romance. Often these feelings are experienced when a new relationship is beginning. The question is whether romance is possible for long-term marriages.

Often, when two people are together for many years, romance seems to leave the marriage. The relationship sometimes deteriorates into two roommates just coexisting under the same roof.

Lack of romance is a common problem for many marriages. Hurt, disappointment and anger have an easy entrance when romance leaves. We might not feel "in love" anymore. But don't despair, because there is hope. Love is a choice, and romance requires continual effort and energy.

There are two major misconceptions regarding romance. The first misconception is that romance is ungodly. Perhaps it is the media's distorted, amoral, permissive presentation of romance which has fostered this attitude. The second misconception is that romance happens immediately or spontaneously!

None of us is a mind-reader. Men in particular need help in expressing their romantic feelings. They need encouragement, specifics and direction. Romance takes some thought, some work and some time. Spouses should nurture their mutual physical attraction – to do the best with what they have – giving special attention to weight, nutrition, exercise, hygiene and dressing attractively.

Romance is also inspired when we express love verbally. We should not assume that our mates already know that we love them just because of the things we do for them. Love needs to be verbalized. Giving caring compliments and reinforcing the positive characteristics of our spouse help to prevent taking each other for granted.

Touching one another affectionately during the day – not just at bedtime – also encourages romance. As human beings, we all require affection. Tenderness, gentleness and kindness are attitudes which enhance romantic behavior. The fruits of the Holy Spirit are very important in this respect. God cares about our having a fulfilling, romantic marriage.

WHAT DESTROYS ROMANCE?

There are actions and behavior which seriously undermine romance in a marriage. Ridicule and sarcasm are two of the most destructive, self-defeating methods of dealing with anger and conflicts. Being unwilling to communicate problems or needs verbally is another hindrance. Don't assume that your mate can read your mind.

A successful relationship takes two people willing to talk, willing to risk being misunderstood and willing to completely open up to each other. Intimacy will not develop if only one person is willing to talk. Invest and schedule your time alone to encourage one-on-one communication. These times are especially important for couples with children. It is vitally important that your marriage relationship be nurtured as well as the children's.

THE IMPORTANCE OF COMPANIONSHIP

Companionship is the sharing and the blending of experiences. A marriage brings two, very different people together with the purpose of making them one. Ideas, thoughts and information should be shared back and forth. Communication is the process of tearing down barriers and walls which may have built up from previous painful experiences.

Companionship also means learning how to deal with conflicts. No close personal relationship is exempt from some level of conflict. Marriage is the blending of two, unique individuals; so there will naturally be conflicts. We can choose to resolve these conflicts constructively and to work through them, or we can blow them out of proportion.

Pride and selfishness are often the culprits which keep us from resolving conflicts and differences with our mates. We must learn to cooperate with each other and to value each other's opinions, abilities and achievements. We should build up our mate's confidence, appreciate his unique qualities and not allow the carnal nature of self-defense and self-preservation to prevail.

THE IMPORTANCE OF MUTUAL SUBMISSION

Serving and servanthood emphasize the spiritual aspects of a marriage. A successful marriage is a spiritual mystery. For two human being to truly come together, the "I'm Number One" attitude must be changed so we can truly serve one another in love. We need to strive for the "agape" love, the unconditional love that always puts the other person first. Given our human nature, this remarkable attitude can only be accomplished through God's Spirit and His grace.

In Ephesians 5, husbands are told to love their wives as Christ loved the Church; and wives are told to submit to their husbands. But the priority must be that both individuals submit themselves to God and to each other as brothers and sisters in the Lord. Therefore, husbands and wives are called to mutual servanthood to and for one another. The message of the Scriptures is that submission is mutual! Problems arise when power becomes an issue.

A SATISFYING SEXUAL RELATIONSHIP

If a couple is working on the aforementioned areas of their relationship, their physical relationship is naturally enhanced. Many married couples experience sexual problems, but often these problems are only symptomatic of communication breakdown or a practical lack of application of godly principles. Very few sexual problems are of a physical origin.

Touching, holding and nurturing each other is very important to a satisfying sexual relationship. There is a lack of candor in Christian circles about sexual relationships. Most people could be having a better sex life if they would just discuss the subject freely with their mates, not putting the blame on each other, but sharing what is pleasing and enjoyable to them. The Song of Solomon is explicit about tender, passionate love-making. Passion and romance is God's norm. We don't need to apologize for such feelings. Let us not allow the world to pollute the beautiful experience God intended love-making to be.

Today, many married couples make sex an end and not a means. They make sex a cause, not an effect.

A CHECKLIST FOR A SUCCESSFUL MARRIAGE

How can a hurting marriage be helped? Here are some questions to consider:

Emotion – What has happened to romance? Has it slipped away? How can romance be renewed?

Companionship – Are we making our ideas, thoughts and needs known to each other? Are we taking personal responsibility for communicating?

Servanthood – Are we nurturing the spiritual aspect of our marriage? Are we serving each other in loving mutuality? Are we nurturing our own individual relationship with God?

Sex – Are we healing past hurts and talking with each other? Do we see the need to give each other fulfillment and pleasure?

Above all, remember that the marriage relationship is rewarding; but "becoming one" is a continual, conscious process. We have a great God who is available for help and healing. Pray together; study the Bible together; encourage each other spiritually; share with each other about spiritual needs and concerns; pray for each other continually. Both partners will grow and mature with mutual fulfillment and satisfaction.

—Condensed from an article from PINE REST TODAY by Dr. Stephen King, M.D. and his wife Judith King, M.S.W.

Dr. Stephen and Judy King are graduates from Christ For The Nations Institute. They have served on staff at Pine Rest Christian Hospital in Grand Rapids, Michigan.

Reprinted by permission: Christ for the Nations CFNI, P.O. Box 769000, Dallas, TX 75376-9000, 800-933-2364

LESSON 11

HOW TO SAVE YOUR MARRIAGE ALONE

MAIN PRINCIPLE

A marriage can be saved, even if it has only one partner who is willing to save it. Godly spouses are promised blessings from the Lord. God can empower us to become the husband and wife He wants us to be.

WHEN CHURCH BELLS AREN'T RINGING

by Susan Raborn

WHAT TO DO WHEN YOUR SPOUSE WON'T GO TO CHURCH

It's 7:15 a.m., and graceful arpeggios gently awaken Cathy from her dreams. She opens her eyes and squints at the alarm clock's red digital display. Her husband, Walter, shifts on his side of the bed, and suddenly Cathy's hand reaches for the radio switch to silence the music.

Cathy remembers that it's Sunday morning. A despondent feeling sinks into the pit of her stomach as she recalls arguing with Walter just before bedtime.

"I slave all week, and on my one day off you want to drag me to church to sing hymns and listen to a preacher talk about God," Walter had fumed. "Well, I don't believe that's the only way to know God. Besides, Sunday is a day of rest – that's in the Bible."

The confrontation had opened old wounds. After Walter had gone to bed, Cathy buried her head in her hands and prayed, "Lord, I praise You for Sunday, a day to worship You. But Lord, will there ever be a day when we can worship You together as a family?"

Cathy sits on the edge of her bed and begins to daydream. She can hear it now: a trumpet blast from the clock radio, followed by a thunderous voice bellowing, "This is the Lord your God, Walter! Today you shall worship Me and not the golf course! This is the day I have made. Rise, Walter, and worship in church with your wife."

Walter jolts out of bed, falling to the floor and repenting for all the times he rejected the command in Scripture to "not give up meeting together, as some are in the habit of doing. . . ." He vows to honor the Lord's Day, and within the hour, Walter leads his wife and young son through the front door toward the glo-rious ringing of the church bells that are calling all God's people to worship.

"Yeah, right!" Cathy whispers, as she stands up and puts on her bathrobe. She gently shuts the bedroom door and walks down the hall to wake up her son.

THE MISSION

A spouse may refuse to attend church for many reasons. If the unchurched spouse is a Christian, that refusal is ultimately a lack of obedience to a clear command of Scripture found in Hebrews 10:24-25. However, when one partner is not attending church, the reason is more likely the outcome of an "unequally yoked" marriage where one partner is not a Christian. Cathy's marriage lacks true biblical unity, and she feels a profound void.

Pastors, church leaders and counselors hear the same story over and over: "My spouse won't go to church with me. What do I do?" Hopefully, anyone in a counseling position will respond with caring biblical advice. But it's interesting how often we skip over a fundamental issue: What is the Christian spouse's own walk with Christ like?

Now some may be objecting: Wait a minute! I love the Lord, and I want my spouse to love Him as much as I do.

That's good, but what is the motivation behind wanting your spouse to love the Lord? Is it to have peace in the home instead of hostility? To raise up children in the will and admonition of the Lord? To have spiritual intimacy? To save your marriage? To be assured of your spouse's eternal destiny?

These things are by no means improper goals, but

concentrating on the problems distracts from our mission, which is to glorify God in any situation. By doing that, we will develop a deeper acceptance of His sovereignty, even if that means the spouse never accepts Christ.

So, how does this apply to real life?

THE CASE OF THE UNCHURCHED CHRISTIAN

A Christian is to be in the body of believers. Using his or her gifts to serve others and getting exposure to the instruction of God's Word. Anyone who professes to be a Christian but does not attend church is disregarding God's Word and thus is living outside His will.

In addition to obeying God's desire that we worship Him, there are a couple practical reasons why the non-attending Christian should attend church:

- **We are all given spiritual gifts to encourage and support each other as we live for the Lord.** If any one of us stays away from church, we miss out on serving our family in Christ (1 Peter 4:10-11). Troubles will come our way, but if we are faithful in assembling with other believers and ministering to them, we will have plenty of resources and help in our own times of need.

- **God calls His people to worship in unity.** Like a parent at a family gathering, God is truly blessed when His family comes together before Him. When some, like the prodigal's elder brother, refuse to come and rejoice, it pains the Father and detracts from the fellowship. Perhaps the most tragic aspect is that estrangement from God's family can't help but distance one from God Himself.

    Churchgoing spouses must prayerfully beware of condescending language in the guise of "loving confrontation." In the end, actions will always speak louder than words. If we talk of love and fellowship but our tone and actions don't reflect those virtues, our actions will drown out any spoken words with an all-too-familiar resonance: hypocrisy. But when we allow the Holy Spirit to work, miracles happen.

THE CASE OF THE UNBELIEVING SPOUSE

Unfortunately, a marriage with an unbelieving spouse seems destined to stay spiritually void week after week, month after month. Years of persistent prayer on the part of the believing spouse may produce little change in the behavior of the unbeliever.

Christians must remember that the focus should be on Christ, not on winning a spouse to the Lord. Ironically, letting go by keeping our focus upward and praising God for our salvation is the most effective basis for maintaining a compelling testimony of hope.

So, how does someone like Cathy live with a non-Christian partner? According to 1 Peter 3:1-7, she is to live so that her husband sees her life as glorifying to God. Here are some ways she can do that:

- **Concentrate on winning the spouse without a word.** A spouse can be won by one action, whereas a thousand of the most eloquent and compelling words may fall lifeless to the ground. And that is where only the Holy Spirit can save us — and the unbelieving spouse — from ourselves. By action, we don't mean putting Bible verses on golf clubs, the mirror, in the lunch box, or even on those beer bottles.

    What will win his or her heart are Christlike acts of submission. The great danger is leaving the spouse feeling as if you'd rather be married to some "wonderful Christian." Nor do you want to volunteer to run hot meals for needy church friends if that means leaving your spouse home alone with a TV dinner.

- **Submit yourselves, one to another.** "Does that mean I have to miss church and drive up to the lake with him?" Ironically, you could very well be honoring God through such submission. Refusing to budge from church attendance for a weekend away or to go to an occasional Sunday brunch is ultimately a power play that can only harm a marriage by driving a wedge between the spouse and "religion."

    Such intolerance shows a lack of wisdom and maturity as a believer. While a believer's consistent absence from the body is harmful, a legalistic lack of grace is "un-Christian."

- **Pray for the salvation of your spouse.** God is the master of all, and Scripture is replete with examples of His working in spite of, and even through, the shortcomings of His servants. Characteristically, whenever He intervenes it is in the context of sincere prayer. God's people come to Him on their knees and He lifts them up. Of all the words and deeds one might wisely pursue to win a spouse to Christ, the deeds of prayerful words lifted up before God will always be the most productive. Pray without ceasing.

Cathy sits beside her sleeping 8-year-old son, gently running her fingers through his blond bangs. She silently prays, "Father God – my husband is in Your hands." She smiles and gently rocks the boy's shoulders.

"Ben. . . . time to get up."

Ben's eyes flutter open, and he looks into his mother's face.

"It's time to go to church," says Cathy.

"Is Dad going with us?" Ben asks, rubbing his eyes.

"No, not today, but maybe one day. We'll just keep praying."

"Oh," Ben replies, with a tinge of sadness.

"I know," says his mom. "But let's get ready. We don't want to be late."

— Focus on the Family magazine, January 1996. Used by permission: Author Susan Raborn

I AM...!

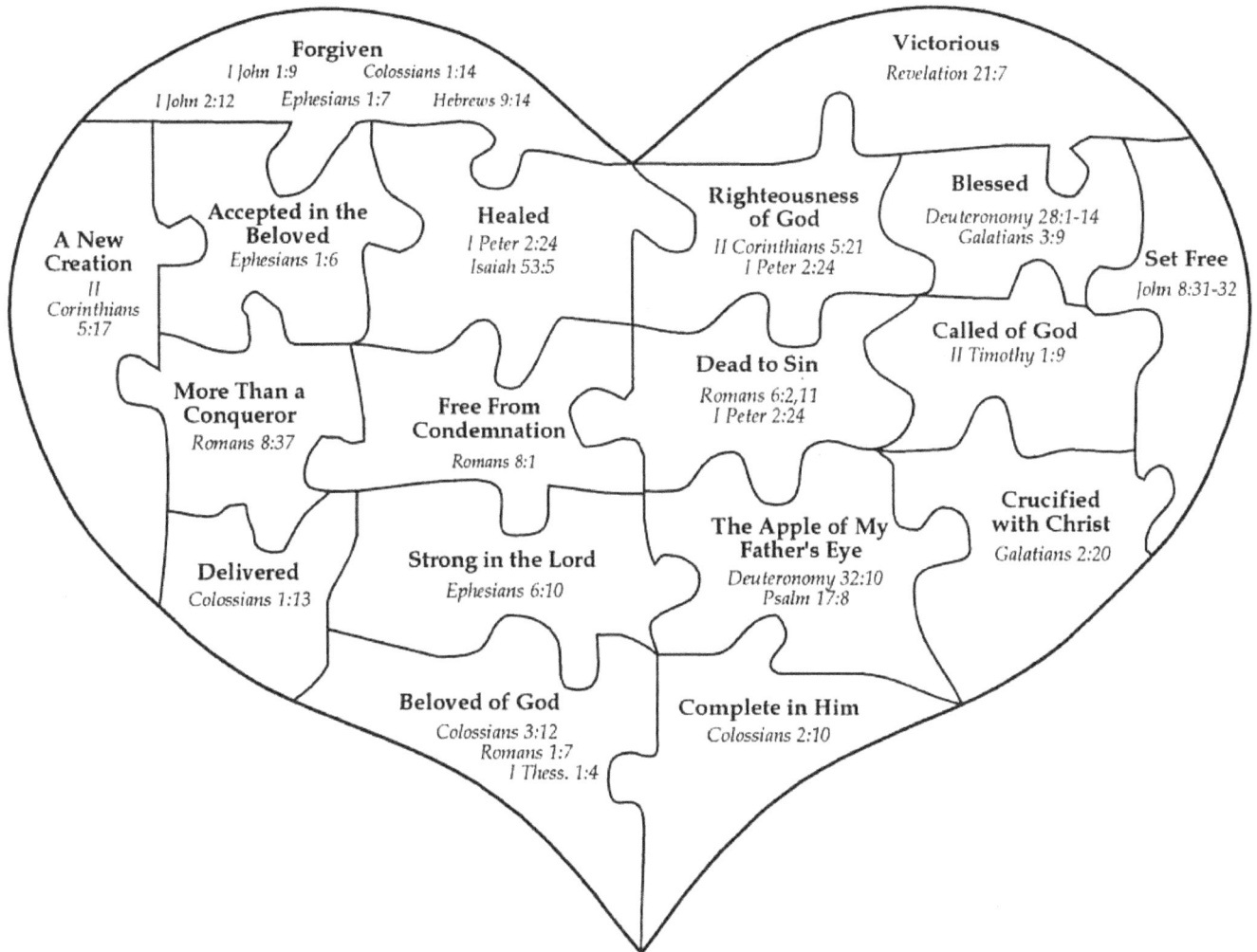

LESSON 12

SERVING GOD TOGETHER

MAIN PRINCIPLE

God has a plan for our marriage and ministry together.
God will reveal His plan for us as we walk in the Spirit
together. He can empower us to become the husband
and wife He wants us to be.

SERVING GOD TOGETHER

1. Do a character study of a couple found in Scripture. Read between the lines of Scripture and imagine what principles motivated your chosen Bible couple. Be ready to share the principles by which you think this couple lived and ministered together.

2. Identify biblical principles by which you think God is asking you to live as a couple serving Him together in the future.

FUNDAMENTALS OF A CHRISTIAN MARRIAGE

by Dr. James Dobson

We live in an age when many statistics reveal almost half of marriages end in divorce, and within the Church there seems to be no exception. Something has to be fundamentally wrong with the way our generation interprets this sacred union which was divinely designed to bring stability to our lives, our families and ultimately society as a whole. In this excerpt from Dr. Dobson's first book on marriage, the fundamental factors required for a successful marriage are described in the three "C's" of: A Christ-Centered Home, Commitment and Communication.

In an effort to draw on the experiences of those who have successfully lived together as husbands and wives, some years ago we asked married couples to participate in an informal study. More than six hundred people agreed to speak candidly to the younger generation about the concepts and methods that have worked in their homes. They each wrote comments and recommendations, which were carefully analyzed and compared. The advice they offered is not new, but it certainly represents a great place to begin. In attempting to learn any task, one should start with the fundamentals—those initial steps from which everything else will later develop. In this spirit, our panel of six hundred offered three tried-and-tested, back-to-basics recommendations with which no committed Christian would likely disagree.

A CHRIST-CENTERED HOME

The panel first suggested that newlyweds establish and maintain a Christ-centered home. Everything rests on that foundation. If a young husband and wife are deeply committed to Jesus Christ, they enjoy enormous advantages over a family with no spiritual dimension. A meaningful prayer life is essential in maintaining a Christ-centered home. Of course, some people use prayer the way they follow their horoscopes, attempting to manipulate an unidentified "higher power." One of my friends teasingly admits that he utters a prayer each morning on the way to work when he passes the doughnut shop. He knows it is unhealthy to eat the greasy pastries, but he loves them dearly. Therefore, he asks the Lord for permission to indulge himself each day. He'll say, "If it is Your will that I have a doughnut this morning, let there be a parking space available as I circle the block." If no spot can be found for his car, he circles the block and prays again.

Shirley and I have taken our prayer life a bit more seriously. In fact, this communication between man, woman and God has been the stabilizing factor throughout our forty-plus years of married life. In good times, in hard times, in moments of anxiety, and in periods of praise, we have shared this wonderful privilege of talking directly to our heavenly Father. What a concept. No appointment is needed to enter into His presence. We don't have to go through His subordinates or bribe His secretaries. He is simply there, whenever we bow before Him.

Some of the highlights of my life have occurred in these quiet sessions with the Lord. At one point, shortly after our daughter Danae earned her driver's license, Shirley and I covenanted between us to pray for our son and daughter at the close of each day. Not only were we concerned about the risk of an automobile accident, but we were also aware of so many other dangers that lurk out there in a city like Los Angeles, where we lived at the time. That part of the world is known for its weirdos, ding-a-lings, and fruitcakes. That's one reason we found ourselves on our knees each evening, asking for divine protection for the teenagers we loved so much.

One night we were particularly tired and collapsed into bed without our benedictory prayer. We were almost asleep before Shirley's voice pierced the night. "Jim," she said, "We haven't prayed for our kids yet today. Don't you think we should talk to the Lord?"

I admit it was very difficult for me to pull my six-foot two-inch frame out of our warm bed that night. Nevertheless, we got on our knees and offered a prayer for our children's safety, placing them in the hands of the Father once more.

Later we learned that Danae and a girlfriend had gone to a fast-food establishment and bought hamburgers and Cokes. They had driven up the road a few miles and were sitting in the car eating the meal when a city policeman drove by, shining his spotlight in all directions. He was obviously looking for someone, but gradually went past.

A few minutes later, Danae and her friend heard a clunk from under the car. They looked at one another nervously and felt a sharp bump. Before they could leave, a man crawled out from under the car and emerged on the passenger side. He was very hairy and looked like he had been on the street for weeks. The man immediately came to the door and attempted to open it. Thank God, it was locked. Danae quickly started the car and drove off...no doubt at record speed.

When we checked the timing of this incident, we realized that Shirley and I had been on our knees at the precise moment of danger. Our prayers were answered. Our daughter and her friend were safe! It is impossible for me to overstate the need for prayer in the fabric of family life. Not simply as a shield against danger, of course. A personal relationship with Jesus Christ is the cornerstone of marriage, giving meaning and purpose to every dimension of living. Being able to bow in prayer as the day begins or ends gives expression to frustrations and concerns, which might not otherwise be ventilated. On the other end of that prayer line is a loving heavenly Father who has promised to hear and answer our petitions. In this day, when families are disintegrating on every side, we dare not try to make it on our own.

Couples who have not found a common faith are often left in a vulnerable position. That brings us to the second back-to-the-basics suggestion for a successful marriage made by our panel of six hundred "experts."

COMMITTED LOVE

Very few certainties touch us all in this mortal existence, but one absolute is that we will experience hardship and stress at some point. Nobody remains unscathed. Life will test each of us severely, if not during younger days, then through the events surrounding our final days.

Jesus spoke of this inevitability when He said to His disciples, "In the world ye shall have tribulation: but be of good cheer; I have overcome the world" John 16:33.

Marriages that lack an iron-willed determination to hang together at all costs are vulnerable not only to the great tragedies of life but also to the daily frustrations that wear and tear on a relationship.

WHAT WILL YOU DO THEN, WHEN UNEXPECTED TORNADOES BLOW THROUGH YOUR HOME?

Minor irritants, when accumulated over time, may be even more threatening to a relationship than catastrophic events. There are times in every good marriage when a husband and wife just don't like each other very much. There are occasions when they feel as though they will never love their partner again. Emotions are like that. They flatten out occasionally, like an automobile tire with a nail in the tread. Riding on the rim is a pretty bumpy experience for everyone on board. What will you do then, when unexpected tornadoes blow through your home, or when the doldrums leave your sails sagging and silent? Will you pack it in? Will you pout and cry and seek ways to strike back? Or will your commitment hold you steady? These questions must be addressed now, before Satan has an opportunity to put his noose of discouragement around your neck. Set your jaw and clench your fists. Nothing short of death must ever be permitted to come between the two of you. *Nothing!*

This attitude is missing from so many marital relationships today.

I read of a wedding ceremony in New York years ago in which the bride and groom each pledged *"to stay with you for as long as I shall love you."* I doubt their marriage lasted even a few years. The *feeling* of love is simply too ephemeral to hold a relationship together for very long. It comes and goes. That's why our panel of six hundred was adamant on this point. They have lived long enough to know that a weak marital commitment will inevitably lead to divorce.

COMMUNICATION

The third recommendation by our panel represents another basic ingredient of good marriages. Like the other two, it begins with the letter C—good communication between husbands and wives. This topic has been beaten to death by writers of marriage books, but I would like to offer some less-over-worked thoughts on marital communication that might be useful to young married couples.

First, it must be understood that males and females differ in yet another way not mentioned earlier. Research makes it clear that most little girls are blessed with greater linguistic ability than most little boys, and it remains a life-long talent. Simply stated, she talks more than he does.

As an adult, she typically expresses her feelings and thoughts far better than her husband and is often irritated by his reticence. God may have given her 50,000 words per day and her husband only 25,000. He comes home from work with 24,975 used up and merely grunts his way through the evening. He may descend into Monday night football, while his wife is dying to expend her remaining 25,000 words.

Erma Bombeck, a female columnist, once proposed in jest that an ordinance be passed stating that *a man who watches 168,000 football games in a single season be declared legally dead.*

> # INABILITY OR UNWILLINGNESS OF HUSBANDS TO REVEAL THEIR FEELINGS TO THEIR WIVES IS ONE OF THE COMMON COMPLAINTS OF WOMEN.

The complexity of the human personality guarantees exceptions to every generalization. Yet any knowledgeable marriage counselor knows that the inability or unwillingness of husbands to reveal their feelings to their wives is one of the common complaints of women. It can almost be stated as an absolute: Show me a quiet, reserved husband and I'll show you a frustrated wife. She wants to know what he's thinking, what happened at the office or jobsite, how he views the children, and especially, how he feels about her. The husband, by contrast, finds some things better left unsaid. It is a classic struggle.

The paradox is that a highly emotional, verbal woman is sometimes drawn to the strong silent type. He seemed so secure and "in control" before they were married. She admired his unflappable nature and his coolness in a crisis. Then they were married, and the flip side of his great strength became obvious. He wouldn't talk! So for the next forty years, she gnashed her teeth because her husband couldn't give what she needed from him. It just wasn't in him.

One familiar song written by Paul Simon in the 60's paints a sobering picture of the person who fears intimacy. Fear of disappointment, pain, or rejection is often the culprit. Attempting to build a relationship with such a person is likely to be a lonely endeavor. Consider the following lyrics which describes the individual who has allowed wounds of the past to altar their capacity to love.

A Winter's Day
©1965 Paul Simon.

In a deep and dark December:
I am alone.
Gazing from my window
To the streets below
On a freshly fallen silent
Shroud of snow.

I am a rock
I am an island.

I've built walls
A fortress deep and mighty.
That none may penetrate.
I have no need of friendship
Friendship causes pain.
Its laughter and its loving I disdain.

I am a rock
I am an island.

Don't talk of love:
Well I've heard the word before;
It's sleeping in my memory.
I won't disturb the slumber of
Feelings that have died.
If I never loved I never
Would have cried.

I am a rock
I am an island.

I have my books
And my poetry to protect me;
I am shielded in my amour,
Hiding in my room,
Safe within my womb.
I touch no one and
No one touches me.

I am a rock
I am an island.

And a rock feels no pain;
And an island never cries.

What is the solution to such communication problems? As always, it involves compromise. A man has a clear responsibility to "cheer up his wife which he hath taken" (Deut. 24:5). He must not claim himself a "rock" who will never allow himself to be vulnerable again. He must press himself to open his heart and share his deeper feelings with his wife. Time must be reserved for meaningful conversations. Taking walks, going out to breakfast, or riding bicycles on a Saturday morning are fresh opportunities for conversation that can help keep love alive. Communication can occur even in families where the husband leans inward and the wife leans outward. In these instances, I believe that the primary responsibility for compromise lies with the husband.

Some women, however, are married to men who will never be able to fully express themselves or understand the feminine needs I have described. Their emotional structure makes it impossible for them to comprehend the feelings and frustrations of another—particularly those occurring in the opposite sex. These men will not read a book such as this and would probably resent it if they did. They have never been required to "give" and have no idea how it is done. What, then, is to be the reaction of their wives? What would you do if your husband lacked the insight to be what you need him to be? My advice is that you change that which can be altered, explain that which can be understood, teach that which can be learned, revise that which can be improved, resolve that which can be settled, and negotiate that which is open to compromise.

Create the best marriage possible from the raw materials brought by two imperfect human beings with two distinctly unique personalities. But for all the rough edges that can never be smoothed and the faults that can never be eradicated, try to develop the best possible perspective and determine in your mind to accept reality exactly as it is. The first principle of mental health is to accept that which cannot be changed. You could easily go to pieces over adverse circumstances that are beyond your control. You can will to hang tough, or you can yield to cowardice. Depression is often evidence of emotional surrender.

Can you accept the fact that your husband will never be able to meet all your needs and aspirations? Seldom does one human being satisfy every longing and hope in another. Obviously, this coin has two sides: you can't be his perfect woman either. He is no more equipped to resolve your entire package of emotional needs than you are to become his sexual dream machine twenty-four hours a day. Both partners have to settle for human foibles, faults, irritability, fatigue and occasional nighttime "headaches." A good marriage is not one in which perfection reigns; it is a relationship in which a healthy perspective overlooks a multitude of unresolvables.

I am especially concerned about the mother of small children who chooses to stay at home as a full-time homemaker. If she looks to her husband as the provider of all adult conversation and the satisfier of every emotional need, their marriage could quickly run aground.

He returns home from work at night somewhat depleted and in need of tranquility, as we discussed earlier. Instead of tranquility, he finds a woman who is continually starved for attention and support. When she sees in his eyes that he has nothing left to give, she becomes either depressed or angry (or both) and he has no idea how he can help her. I understand this feminine need and have attempted to articulate it to men. Nevertheless, a woman's total dependence on a man places too much pressure on the marital relationship. It sometimes cracks under the strain. What can be done, then? A woman with a normal range of emotional needs cannot simply ignore her needs—they scream for fulfillment.

I have long recommended that women in this situation seek to supplement what their husbands can give by cultivating meaningful female relationships. Having girlfriends with whom they can talk heart to heart, study the Scriptures, and share childcare techniques can be vital to mental health. Without this additional support, loneliness and low self-esteem can build and begin to choke the marriage to death. Sadly, this is not always easy to implement.

In recent years we've witnessed a breakdown in relationships between women. A hundred years ago, wives and mothers did not have to seek female friendship. It was programmed into the culture. Women canned food together, washed clothes at the creek together, and cooperated in church charity work together. When babies were born, the mother was visited by aunts, sisters, neighbors, and churchwomen who came to help her diaper, feed and care for the child. An automatic support system surrounded women and made life easier. Its absence translated quickly into marital conflict and can lead to divorce.

To the young wives who are reading these words, I urge you not to let this happen to you. Invest time in your female friends—even though you are busy. Resist the temptation to pull into the walls of your home and wait for your husband to be all things to you. Stay involved as a family in a church that meets your needs and preaches the Word. Remember that you are surrounded by many other women with similar feelings. Find them. Care for them. Give to them. And in the process, your own self-esteem will rise. Then when you are content, your marriage will flourish. It sounds simplistic, but that is the way we were designed by an infinitely wise and loving God.

—James C. Dobson, Ph.D. hosts the radio program Dr. James Dobson's Family Talk. A licensed psychologist and marriage, family, and child counselor, he is a clinical member of the American Association for Marriage and Family Therapy. For 14 years Dr. Dobson was an associate clinical professor of pediatrics at the University of Southern California School of Medicine, and he served for 17 years on the attending staff of Children's Hospital Los Angeles in the Division of Child Development and Medical Genetics. He is the author of more than 30 books. Dr. Dobson resides in Colorado with his wife, Shirley.

Excerpt from the book "Love for a Lifetime" by Dr. James Dobson © 2004 Multnomah Publishers, P.O. Box 1720, Sisters, OR 97759. Used by permission.

ZOE COURSE DESCRIPTIONS

"My sheep hear My voice, and I know them, and they follow Me." John 10:27 (KJV)

HEARING COURSES

Hearing God's Voice

In this course, everyone is encouraged to participate by applying the principles they read in scripture in order to learn to recognize when the Holy Spirit is speaking. The inner knowing, inner voice, and the authoritative voice of the Holy Spirit are discussed, as well as other manifestations of the Holy Spirit. The Lord is personal and unique, and desires to communicate with each one of His sheep in a personal and unique manner! (This course is a prerequisite for all the following courses except for How to Hear God's Voice—In Marriage.)

How To Hear God's Voice—In Christ

In the Hearing God's Voice course we learned how to hear God as individuals, whereas in the In Christ course, we learn how the body of Christ operates together under His direction and to His glory. We look at Romans 12 and examine the motive gifts that determine our individual bents. This study enables us to understand, appreciate and love each other. We also look at the Trinity and how they operate together. We learn about the precious person of the Holy Spirit and how He teaches, guides and comforts us. We also learn about the gifts of the Holy Spirit in 1 Corinthians 12 and 14 brought about as the Holy Spirit moves through us. Participants have remarked that this course has enabled them to see people the way God sees them and how they fit in the body of Christ.

How To Hear God's Voice—In Marriage

This course is based on the love relationship God had with mankind in the very beginning. We examine our attitudes toward each other and how they reflect the greatest love of all, the love of Christ. Do we love and honor each other with the unconditional love that our Lord Jesus had for us while dying on the cross? As in previous classes, we examine scripture, seek the Lord, and ask Him, "How can I better serve and love my spouse?" We discover how we complete each other, not compete with each other.

How To Hear God's Voice—In the Family

In today's society we see the growing deterioration of the family. Parents are confused about what the Bible teaches on family issues. During this course we examine scriptures and what it means to: "Train up a child [early childhood] in the way he should go [and in keeping with his individual bent], and when he is old [teen years can be the best] he will not depart from it." (AMP with additions)

KNOWING COURSES

How To Know God's Voice—In Intimate Friendship

Intimate Friendship with God! Can we experience such a relationship with the Creator of the universe? Here we examine what the Bible teaches us about the fear of the Lord, and how we can, indeed, have a deeper, more intimate relationship with Him. This is a very personal, yet freeing course on growing intimacy with God.

How To Know God's Voice—In Worship

The focus of this course is on ministering to the Lord. During our time together the Lord draws us corporately into His presence as we worship Him. We study what worship is, why we worship, and how we worship.

How To Know God's Voice—In His Presence

The Lord is calling each one of His sheep to come into His presence and to know Him in a deeper way. This course is not for the new believer nor the faint in heart. Those who are serious about knowing the Father in a more intimate way will find this class challenging but rewarding. Examining Jesus' last days on earth will direct us into the presence of the Lord. This class is for those who have completed other ZOE classes.

How To Know God's Voice—In the Coming of the Lord

Many are proclaiming dates and times when the Lord Jesus will return for His bride. This class is designed to focus on our preparation for His coming, not when He is coming, and to better understand the Lord's statement of Revelation 22:20: "Yes, I am coming." It is the goal of this course to prepare ourselves as the bride of Christ, with hearts that will respond with "Amen. Come, Lord Jesus."

FOLLOWING COURSES

How To Follow God's Voice—In Power

Evangelism is often thought of as a bad word! In this course we come to realize that God has a special plan for evangelism for us if we are only sensitive and obedient to His voice. Preparing your testimony, leading someone in salvation, and discipling others are a few of the topics discussed in this course. This is a real life-changer as we minister in "power evangelism!"

How To Follow God's Voice—In Healing

During this course we examine the scriptures in which Jesus healed the sick. The Holy Spirit highlights these passages as we study, and our faith increases! We realize that Jesus is the Healer, and we are simply His vessels as we listen to and follow His voice.

How To Follow God's Voice—In Intercession

Jesus is in constant intercession (Hebrews 7:25). As we come before Him in worship, intercession is a natural outflow of our relationship with Him. By yielding to the Holy Spirit, our ministry to others through intercession will increase.

How To Follow God's Voice—In Spiritual Warfare

As we come to know and recognize who our Lord is, He reveals to us who He is not! The tactics of Satan and our spiritual weapons are defined in this class. The Lord leads us in spiritual warfare as He enlists and mobilizes His army!

ONE-ON-ONE DISCIPLESHIP

Discipleship by the Word of God and the Power of the Holy Spirit

This 12-week course was developed by a disciple-maker after many years of successful one-on-one discipleship. Through this method the Holy Spirit is allowed to minister to the disciple through the Word and the encouragement of the disciple-maker. No other techniques or methods are used.

The entire course has been designed to enable individuals to feel confident in making disciples as directed by our Lord: "Therefore go and make disciples of all nations…." Matthew 28:19.

Not only do participants learn what discipleship means according to the Word of God, but they are encouraged to participate in a one-on-one discipleship program as part of the course. This training allows individuals to take great strides in their personal relationship with God and in ministry. It changes lives in a very simple, yet powerful way.

EVANGELISTIC OUTREACH — MINISTRY IN HOMES

Captivated by Their Character

This series of courses called Captivated by Their Character is designed to reach the unbeliever, new believer, and those needing a refresher course on the Trinity.

They are offered in a non-threatening, home atmosphere where every effort is made to make the participant feel comfortable with the material. For example, everyone uses the same Bible, referring to page numbers rather than books, no reading is required outside of the course, and they are given the freedom to express their inadequacies as a believer or non-believer.

The three 6-week courses in the Captivated by Their Character series are titled Who Is Jesus?, Who Is God the Father? and Who Is the Holy Spirit?

Additional information is available on the website at www.zoeministires.org/zoe-courses

MAGAZINE LIST

For your convenience we have included the following list of magazines from which this course's articles have been drawn. If you wish to receive these magazines on a regular basis, the subscription information below will help.

Charisma and Christian Life
Subscription Service Department
P.O. Box 420234   (800) 829-3346
Palm Coast, FL 32142-0234   www.charismamag.com

Christ for the Nations
P.O. Box 769000   (800) 933-CFNI
Dallas, TX 75376-9000   www.cfni.org

Decision Magazine
Billy Graham Evangelistic Association
P.O. Box 668886   (877) 247-2426
Charlotte, NC 28266-8886   www.bgea.org

Focus on the Family
Magazines / Subscriptions   (800) A-FAMILY (232-6459)
Colorado Springs, CO 80995   www.family.org

Ministry Today Magazine
(formerly Ministries Today)
Charisma Media
600 Rinehart Road   (407) 333-7100
Lake Mary, FL 32746   www.ministrytodaymag.com

www.ingramcontent.com/pod-product-compliance
Lightning Source LLC
Chambersburg PA
CBHW081153090426
42736CB00017B/3307